TAG RUGBY

2ND EDITION

TAG RUGBY

EVERYTHING YOU NEED TO KNOW TO PLAY AND COACH

2ND EDITION

JANE LIDDIARD

BLOOMSBURY

LONDON • NEW DELHI • NEW YORK • SYDNEY

Published by Bloomsbury Publishing Plc
50 Bedford Square
London WC1B 3DP
www.bloomsbury.com

First edition 2014

ISBN (print): 978-1-4081-9536-9
ISBN (ePdf): 978-1-4729-0802-5
ISBN (EPUB): 978-1-4081-9537-6

Acknowledgements
Cover photographs, top left and bottom © Andrew Redlington – RFU/ The RFU Collection/Getty Images; top right © Photofusion/Universal Images Group/Getty Images
Inside photographs © The Bridge, with exceptions listed on page 7
Illustrations by Dave Saunders
Commissioned by Kirsty Schaper

This book is produced using paper that is made from wood grown in managed, sustainable forests. It is natural, renewable and recyclable. The logging and manufacturing processes conform to the environmental regulations of the country of origin.

Typeset in 10pt on 15pt Myriad Pro by Margaret Brain, Wisbech, Cambs
Printed and bound in China by C&C Offset Printing Co
10 9 8 7 6 5 4 3 2 1

CONTENTS

For my granddaughter Francesca

ACKNOWLEDGEMENTS

With thanks to my editor Kirsty Schaper at Bloomsbury for her help and encouragement; to Imogen Gaunt and Callum Sheppard at Harlequins RFC for their help; and to Jon Burton, former head coach of tag rugby at Salisbury RFC, for his information and advice.

Special thanks go to my husband John for his wonderful patience and unflagging support; Crown copyright material for the National Curriculum is reproduced with the permission of the Controller of HMSO and the Queen's Printer for Scotland.

PICTURE CREDITS

PREFACE

The second edition of this popular book contains the most up-to-date rules of play, equipment, exercises and drills, fun and games, tips for coaches and referees, funding and festivals, information about the professional game, and much more.

Rugby has become increasingly popular since England won the World Cup in 2003 and there will certainly be a resurgence of interest again for the eighth Rugby World Cup in 2015, especially as it is being held in England.

Community rugby begins with tag rugby, which can be played safely by girls and boys together as young as five years old. Players then progress to junior and senior rugby, and for the really talented players there is the chance of a place at a rugby academy and then on to the professional game.

The stars of the future depend on this enthusiasm for the game at club and school level. Enthusiasm really is vital for instilling a love of playing the game, as well as for bringing on gifted players. Tag rugby coaches and teachers, both the absolute beginners and those with knowledge of how to play the game, will find this book invaluable. Using clear, simple language, diagrams, exercises and games, as well as lesson plans, all based on the RFU's own rules and instructions, this book will guide you through tag rugby step by step. There are also chapters on refereeing, guidelines for working with children, and health and safety as well as essential information for starting up a club or school team, entering festivals and competitions, playing at local and professional grounds on match days and finding extra funds.

This book will improve your coaching and playing skills and, above all, ensure that tag rugby is immensely enjoyed by both players and spectators alike.

1 WHAT IS TAG RUGBY?

Tag rugby is a safe, non-contact, easy-to-play evasion game suitable for both adults and children, but this book deals with 'mini' tag rugby for Under-8 girls and boys, playing together in the same side, in primary schools and community clubs. It is aimed at teachers (National Curriculum Key Stages 1 and 2), coaches and referees, as well as parents or carers, but is also a good read for anyone interested in playing or watching tag rugby.

Tag rugby is a sport that's suitable for very young children. There are no scrums, no line-outs and no kicking. In the past, young children and their parents have been put off by injuries caused by scrums, mauls and lineouts; such physical activities are now seen as dangerous and inappropriate for young, growing bodies so a primary school/local community version of mini rugby has been specifically devised by the RFU (Rugby Football Union). The enthusiasm of young children will more than make up for their lack of stature, and the game is particularly beneficial for all-round fitness, running and handling skills, fostering team spirit and becoming a good sport. These running and passing skills are vital in the junior and senior game at all levels and will help players of tag rugby to move through the transitional stages to senior rugby.

Midi rugby is the next section up from mini or tag rugby, and is sometimes called transitional rugby. It allows some contact and prepares you for stepping up to youth rugby.

So what's different from the senior game?

In the senior game the emphasis is very much on physical strength as well as skill and even the backs have very strong physiques now. If you've ever watched a scrum, you can't help but gasp when the referee orders 'Engage!' and the two opposing sides hurl themselves forward to lock neck and shoulders in the front rows. The sheer force of this bone-crunching action always makes me grateful that I'm not in that front row myself! The back row players also have very powerful physiques and the days of the skinny winger are over. Players in the professional game have to withstand the physicality of rucks and mauls and frequently suffer injuries, but these are mostly minor in the form of bruising and cuts. However, it's fair to say that serious injuries sometimes do occur. It's part of the game but, however exciting these aspects of the game appear to very young players, they are only suitable for adults who spend a great deal of their time training to develop their bodies to withstand such pressure and battering. Young children, whose bones are immature and easily broken, cannot risk injury in this way. Therefore, any part of senior rugby which is considered to be a risk for injury has been taken out of the game for minis.

By avoiding physical contact altogether the fear factor of getting hurt has been removed from tag rugby and this is so important because it allows young players to enjoy the excitement of the game in relative safety. They can become part of England's fantastic rugby tradition, getting a taste and enthusiasm for the game which will carry over into junior and then senior rugby. Being part of a club or school team is important for the sport because mini and junior rugby will bring youngsters with a particular talent through to the academies and, hopefully, to a professional career. Professional clubs all have their own academies and most of these academy players go on to play for their clubs. It's a great source of talent for the premiership and other leagues and, of course, for the players it's a way of getting into professional rugby at the highest level.

Even if young players don't become the talented few, they can go on to play rugby at community club level or simply become passionate supporters, which is just as vital for the success of the game at regional, national and international levels. For example, it was very inspiring to see junior rugby players madly practising their goal kicks the day after Jonny

Wilkinson's drop goal secured victory for England in the 2003 Rugby World Cup: they were all dreaming of being future World Cup winners. When international tournaments are being played, such as the Six Nations or the Rugby World Cup, there's always a surge of interest in this sport.

How is it played?

Tag rugby is a non-contact rugby game played between two teams on a rectangular pitch with the aim of scoring tries. The rules are discussed in more detail in Chapter 2 (see pages 23–37). An overall view is as follows.

The numbers for each team are 4 a side for Under 7s on a 12m × 20m sized pitch, and six a side for Under 8s on a 22m × 45m pitch. Tries are scored by running with the ball from your own half of the pitch into the opposition's half, passing to a fellow team player if necessary, and crossing over the opposition's try line, carrying the ball in both hands without being stopped by having your tag taken. Taking a tag, or tagging, is the equivalent of being tackled. Players must carry the ball in both hands because they're less likely to drop it, and also it doesn't leave a hand free for the temptation of fending off or pushing another player away.

Under 8s may go to ground when scoring a try but Under 7s may not. Under 7s tries are scored by grounding the ball with downward pressure with both hands on the ball and both feet on the ground, or simply by running across the try line with the ball in both hands – it's as simple as that. The playing surface is usually the decider. If it's hard, such as concrete or tarmac, or there is a fence or wall boundary, it's safer not to bend over to ground the ball. In this case, crossing the line is sufficient for a try to be scored. However, whatever the surface being played on, even if it is fairly soft, for safety reasons players must not dive over the try line as they do in senior rugby. *They must stay on their feet and bend down to score a try.*

If players do dive over the line or drop to the ground the try is not allowed and a free pass is awarded to the opposing side. The exception to this is if the referee adjudges that the player was illegally knocked over by another player, or was involved in an accidental collision, or slipped when trying to ground the ball, in which case a try may be awarded. Referees should always seek to play advantage and keep the game free-flowing.

The rugby ball must be passed behind or laterally (straight across) to another player when the ball carrier is running towards the opponent's goal line. The ball must not be handed to another player, and the player who has caught the ball must continue play with both hands on the ball.

The ball may not be passed to a player who is in front of the ball carrier; this is known as a 'forward pass'. A forward pass results in a penalty being awarded and this is a free pass to the opposing side.

BUT IT'S FUN TO DIVE!

It's only fun if you know how to do it properly and you are an adult mature and fit enough to withstand a battering. Young bones break easily and internal injuries could occur so this rule prevents any 'glory seeking' and protects mini tag rugby players from injury. This is based on sound medical advice and isn't intended to spoil the enjoyment of the game.

When a player fumbles the ball forwards while attempting to catch it, it's called a 'knock-on'. For Under 7s, knock-ons are allowed in order to keep the game flowing. However, this knock-on rule does not apply to Under 8s. A knock-on by Under 8s will result in a penalty free pass to the opposing side.

For both age groups when a free pass is given the opposing side must retreat 3m towards their own try line. For the attacking side no free passes may be taken within 3m of an opponent's try line so if the offence occurs in this area the player taking the free pass must go back to the 3m line before giving the pass. Once the ball has been picked up and play resumed the passing rules must be observed, which means no forward passing.

A player may only run with the ball if she or he has not been tagged. Once they have been tagged (that is, when their tag has been taken by an opposing player), they have to stop running immediately and pass the ball within three seconds. Failure to do this will result in the ball being given to the opposing side where the offence took place.

It should be remembered that this level of tag rugby is an introduction to the game. This means that coaches and referees may be more flexible and tolerant in their approach to infringements. Giving the benefit of the doubt, allowing play to continue as often as possible, and keeping the whistleblowing to a minimum is essential to ensure a free-flowing

Correct grounding of the ball over the try line

game without constant stopping and starting. If players aren't deliberately infringing in order to gain advantage then play should be allowed to continue. When offences do take place this should result in the non-offending team gaining possession of the ball and continuing the game.

TAG!

Each player wears two tags, one on either side of his or her waist on a belt, as shown below. The tags are attached to the belt by Velcro strips and are easy to grab. If a player's tag is detached by an opposing player the tagger must shout 'Tag!' and hold up the tag as evidence. The referee will shout 'Tag pass!' and the tagged player must then stop running with the ball. If no infringement has taken place, the game will be restarted from where the tagging took place by the player who was tagged. The player must stand still and pass the ball within three seconds. If, however, an infringement has been committed by the tagged player's team, the ball is passed to the defending side and the game is restarted with a free pass from where the offence took place.

Players wearing tags and tag belt

The tags are made of strips of strong material, natural or synthetic, which may be in a team's colours or carry the logo of a sponsor. Each team should have a different coloured tag from their opponents for easy identification.

There is no physical contact of any kind in tag rugby. Physical contact is defined as grabbing hold of an opponent, bringing them down, pulling at a shirt or fending off with an arm or

hand. The ball carrier can only be legitimately stopped by his or her tag being taken by an opponent.

The changes and new rules of play for Mini Tag Under 7s and Under 8s are in Chapter 2 (see pages 23–37), but the following will give you an overview of the game.

HOW MANY PLAYERS?

For the Under 7s there should be four a side, and for Under 8s there should be six a side. There must be the same number of players on each side. Once players get used to the rules, it should be possible for teams at a community club that are not playing in a competition to organise themselves to play a game of tag rugby without a teacher or club trainer refereeing all the time.

PITCH SIZE

The Under 7s play on a pitch size which is 12m × 20m maximum, and the Under 8s on a pitch size 22m × 45m.

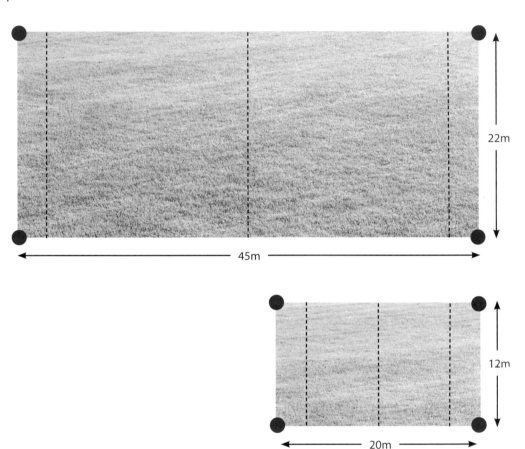

These pitches are rectangular with try lines at both ends of the pitch, a line 3m in from the try lines at either end of the pitch, and a centre line where play begins at the very start of the game, and is started again after play is resumed following a try. No goalposts are needed as there are no kicks of any kind and no goals to be scored. Note that the size of the pitch is related to the age of the players and not to the numbers in the teams.

A tag rugby pitch can be set up on its own specifically for tag rugby use if the club has enough space but if not, and play has to be on a senior rugby pitch, the new pitch size will slot easily across the width of senior pitches. Indeed, several tag rugby pitches can be used in this way along the length of the senior pitch at any one time. Supporters at professional club matches are quite used to seeing several tag rugby matches played across the width of the pitch at half-time in tag rugby competitions. Plastic markers of any kind, including those used in the professional game for training and pre-match warm-ups, can be set down to establish the try lines and sidelines. It's not necessary to have white lines marked out.

The standard dimensions for the Under 7s and Under 8s, rather than the previous system of having varying pitch size options, solve the problem of playing other schools and clubs where the pitch dimensions may have been different from those your club or school were used to. Players can no longer be at a disadvantage by playing on an unfamiliar sized pitch.

2
THE RULES OF TAG RUGBY

This chapter lists the rules as set out by the RFU.

The 'New Rules of Play' were introduced in 2012 after a trial based on research commissioned by the RFU, who were keen to ensure that mini rugby should be played in the best possible way by young children, ensuring minimum risk of injury, simple rules, and above all enjoyment of the game. The RFU developed a brief in 2007 for this research and Exeter University was commissioned to carry it out. The overall results were that too much time spent on drills and coaching reduced playing time and was counter-productive. At mini level children learn best by doing and skills and techniques will develop more naturally and effectively during play, where they can see the results of their efforts rather than running up and down a pitch engaging in long exercises.

However, exercises and games can be fun too if approached with the right attitude of encouragement, praise and humour, and they help to improve fitness. The emphasis should be on enjoyment and love of the game rather than ruthless drilling to become champions.

Teaching children to be overly triumphant is very unpleasant and shouting that they're rubbish and need to do better is a negative approach that will lead more to disappointment and a sense of failure than to any improvement. Yet this doesn't mean that you can't point out where things went wrong or could be improved. Nor does it mean that you can't strive to become champions, but it's how you do it that is so important. Positive enthusiasm and sensitive coaching will bring in the results just the same. Remember, these are small children doing their best, not hopeful adults trying to keep their place in a professional team.

Positivity and enthusiasm can be developed through playing games and fun drills. See Chapter 6 (pages 95–113) for examples.

Emphasis on enjoyment

The greatest emphasis in tag rugby must be on enjoyment while progressing through all levels from minis to senior rugby, rather than establishing a highly competitive culture. It will ensure that the game retains its players because they genuinely enjoy playing and are interested in the game and not subject to the ruthless selection of the best players for teams devoted only to gaining trophies. While some young players will naturally want to feel challenged and competitive, there will always those who don't push themselves forward and they also need to feel that they are doing well whatever their level of skills and experience. Otherwise, they will lose heart and drift away from the game. Senior rugby can only thrive if there are enough players at all team levels to keep the community clubs going.

Tries and scoring

The object of tag rugby is to score more tries than the other team. Scoring tries is the only method of winning points in tag rugby: there are no goalposts and no kicking of any kind is allowed.

HOW MANY POINTS IS A TRY WORTH?

In tag rugby it is recommended that a try is worth five points. Totalling up five points each time a try is scored may amass many points for one side and dishearten the other, so coaches may consider switching players between teams if it isn't a competition or tournament.

HOW ARE TRIES SCORED?

Tries are scored by placing the ball on the ground behind the opponents' try line using downward pressure, with the ball in both hands and the player on his or her feet for Under 7s, or grounding (but not diving) with the ball for Under 8s. After a try has been scored the game is restarted from the centre of the pitch with a free pass by the team that did not score the try (see below for more information on free passes).

RULES FOR SCORING TRIES

When a player crosses the opponents' try line he or she must:

1   be carrying the ball in both hands.

2   place it on the ground with both hands if Under 7s; if Under 8s they can go to ground, but must not dive over the line. Note that grounding the ball is not necessary on hard surfaces or playing areas that have potential hazards. In these instances, crossing the try line is the equivalent of scoring a try by grounding the ball.

3   stay on his/her feet – no diving.

4   have both tags intact, or if tagged have taken only one stride across the goal line.

Any infringement of the above four rules will result in a free pass being given to the opposing team.

HARD SURFACES

If the game is being played on a hard surface such as concrete or tarmac, or there is very restricted space beyond the try line due to a boundary such as a wall or fencing, this is a potential hazard and could cause injury. In this case the ball does not have to be grounded. Instead, players may score a try simply by crossing the goal line with the ball held in both hands, which allows them to stay on their feet, keep their head up and avoid running into any obstacles.

Allowed

- If a player is tagged but grounds the ball legally over the try line within one stride, a try is awarded.

- Going to ground to score a try for Under 8s (but not Under 7s).

Correct grounding of the ball over the try line

Not allowed

- A player can take no more than one step to ground the ball over the try line if tagged. If a player takes more than one stride the try is not allowed and a free pass will be given to the other side.

- Grounding the ball with one hand: players must use both hands to hold the ball at all times.

- Diving over the try line: this looks great in senior rugby but could result in injury for very young players, which is why it is not allowed in tag rugby.

- A ball-carrying player, who is trying to score a try, fending or handing off an opponent who is attempting a tag. No physical contact is permitted even when trying to avoid being tagged. The only way a player can avoid being tagged is by running faster than their opponent, or dodging out of the way without barging into anyone else.

- No snatching of the ball from another player.

Diving onto the ground to score a try is not allowed

All of these offences result in a free pass being given to the opposing team. Most free passes are taken from where the infringement occurred, but for try line infringements or other offences within 7m of the try line, the free pass is taken 7m from the try line. This is so that the team awarded the free pass is not pinned back on their try line to restart the game.

AFTER A TRY IS SCORED

After a try has been scored, the game is restarted with a free pass from the centre of the pitch by the non-scoring side. The player may not run with the ball at the restart, but must pass it to another player, not more than 2m away, by throwing it backwards before moving. Handing the ball to another player is not allowed.

Ball play

Ball play – that is, any handling of the rugby ball during play – is probably the single most important skill for young players to learn for their development to junior and senior levels of the game.

PASSING

Allowed

● Backward and lateral passing (level passing sideways) are permitted.

Passing the ball backwards is allowed

Not allowed

● A forward pass, which is passing the ball to a player who is ahead of the ball carrier.

● Handing the ball to another player: the ball must be thrown.

● Knocking or grabbing the ball out of the hands of the ball carrier.

● Knocking on is an offence for Under 8s but not Under 7s: a knock-on occurs when a player throws, drops or knocks the ball forward.

● Being offside: this can only occur at the restart immediately after a tag. All players from the tagger's team must retreat towards their try line so as not to interfere with the restart pass.

All of these infringements result in a free pass being awarded to the opposing team, unless advantage occurs for the opposing team, in which case play continues.

Passing the ball forwards is not allowed

Passing the ball laterally is allowed

FREE PASSES

Free passes are taken by standing still and when the referee shouts 'Play!' passing the ball behind or laterally to another team player not more than 2m away. The pass must not be taken until the referee gives the signal that everyone is ready to play by shouting 'Play!'

There are four reasons for a free pass being taken:

- To start the game or match at the beginning of each half.

- To restart the game or match after a try has been scored.

- If the ball has gone into touch at the side of the pitch (that is, off the pitch over one of the sidelines).

- When an infringement has occurred.

How to take a free pass

The ball carrier must throw the ball to a player no more than 2m away. The receiver of the pass must start running. The opposing team's players must be 7m back from the mark where the free pass is being taken. They cannot start moving forwards until the ball leaves the hands of the player taking the free pass.

Not allowed

- The player taking the free pass may not run with the ball: the ball must be passed to another player with a backwards pass before he or she moves.

- Handing the ball to another player.

- The receiver not being within 2m of the player taking the free pass.

- The opposing team moving forwards before the free pass has been taken.

KNOCK-ONS – UNDER 7S

Knock-ons, when the ball goes forward by being passed, dropped, or knocked forward accidentally, are not an infringement in the Under 7s game.

KNOCK-ONS – UNDER 8S

For Under 8s knock-ons result in a free pass to the opposing side where the offence took place.

Offside

Tagging: removing the tag

Removing a tag is the equivalent of a tackle in senior rugby. The players wear two tags, one on either side of the waist, so one of them may be removed by an opposing player holding on to it and pulling. The Velcro strips allow the tag to be removed easily and without excessive force. When a tag has been removed, the tagger must hold up the tag and shout 'Tag!' The referee then responds with 'Tag pass!' which means that all players must stop running and the tagged player must take the free pass within three seconds.

After a tag has been removed, the tagger must hold up the tag and shout 'Tag!'

AFTER THE TAG IS REMOVED

When one of their tags has been removed, the ball carrier must:

- attempt to stop as soon as possible. The RFU states that this should be within three strides if possible, but the ball can be passed as the ball carrier is stopping.

- pass the ball within three seconds of being tagged; this includes stopping time.

- if going for a try after being tagged, take only one stride to step over the try line.

- retrieve his or her tag as soon as the ball has been passed and attach it before resuming play.

The ball carrier may not:

- resume the game without reaffixing their tag.

- snatch the tag back from the tagger.

When removing an opponent's tag, the tagger must:

- move back towards his or her try line if within a metre of the tagged player, to allow space for the free pass to be taken.

- hand the tag back to the player once the ball has been passed.

The tagger may not:

- continue to play and influence the game until the tag has been handed back and reaffixed.

- throw the tag down and carry on playing.

Infringements

Any infringement should result in a free pass being awarded to the opposing team from the place where the infringement occurred. All of these infringements have been mentioned above, but are included together below in one section to make them easier to identify.

A) FORWARD PASSING

Forward passing occurs when the player receiving the ball is ahead of the player throwing the ball. 'Forward' is defined as 'moving in the direction of the opponent's goal line'.

B) KNOCK-ON

There is no knock-on for Under 7s. For Under 8s a knock-on occurs when a player does not retain possession in both hands and the ball falls to the ground. It is not always necessary, however, to blow the whistle for this offence if advantage can be played. The non-offending team may be able to pick up the ball and run with it, thereby gaining tactical or territorial advantage.

C) OFFSIDE

A player can only be offside immediately after a player has been tagged. Offside occurs if he or she is not behind the ball and is interfering with play. Once a tag has been made, all players from the tagged team must retreat towards their own try line behind the ball. The non-ball-carrying team should not be penalised, however, if all their players haven't had time to retreat, provided that they are not interfering with play. 'Interfering with play' is when an offside player intercepts or slows down the immediate pass from the tagged player. If this occurs, a free pass should be awarded to the tagged player.

However, a player *can* run from an onside position to intercept the ball. In this case there is no infringement and play continues with the team who made the turnover retaining the ball.

D) DROPPING OR DIVING ONTO THE GROUND

In tag rugby players must stay on their feet in order to play the game. Safety and enjoyment are the keys to successful play, so avoid:

- dropping to the ground with the ball in your hands.

- diving on top of a loose ball on the ground.

- diving over the try line to score a try.

A free pass should be awarded to the opposing team for any of these infringements, although if they occur accidentally the referee may adjudge that continuing play is more desirable than a constant start-stop.

If the ball goes to ground through a missed pass, a player from either team may pick up the ball provided he or she stays on his or her feet. The only occasion when the ball cannot be picked up from the ground to resume the game is when it goes out of play by going into touch. This will result in a free pass for the team that was not carrying the ball at the time of the infringement.

E) KICKING THE BALL

No kicking of any kind is allowed in tag rugby.

F) PHYSICAL CONTACT

Such an infringement occurs when a player:

- hands off another player by pushing out a hand towards that player's face or body. Both hands should be on the ball and no handing off is allowed.

- fends off a player by pushing his or her hand out of the way when an attempted tag is taking place. Both hands should be on the ball and no fending off is allowed.

- barges or accidentally runs into another player.

- grabs the clothing of another player.

- tries to hold on to another player in any way.

- pushes another player away.

- brings another player down to the ground.

- tries to grab the ball from an opposing player or knocks it out of the opposing player's hands.

G) BALL OUT OF PLAY

The ball goes out of play when the ball carrier steps on or runs over the boundary lines of the pitch, or if the ball itself lands on the line or goes outside the boundaries of the pitch. A free pass is taken inside the playing area from the point where the ball went out of play. However, note that if the ball goes out of play over the try line, the free pass is taken 7m from the goal line.

Know these rules!

It is important that you and the players know these rules and abide by the same set of rules. However, in the interests of a free-flowing game the referee should not stop play for every little infringement. The RFU's emphasis is on enjoyment rather than slick play. In any case, tag rugby is fast and skilful and it's impossible to spot everything that's going on. Also, minor infringements that don't interfere with play are probably best ignored so that the game can flow. Play advantage wherever possible. This will also ensure that the players don't get disheartened by being constantly penalised and that they don't lose their concentration.

THE RULES IN A NUTSHELL

1. The field of play to be within RFU's set limits.

2. An equal number of players should be on each team: 4 for Under 7s, 6 for Under 8s.

3. A try (scored over try line) is worth 5 points.

4. The player with the ball must pass behind or laterally.

5. Removing a tag is the equivalent of a tackle.

6. A tag results in a free pass by the tagged player within three seconds.

7. The tagged player must then retrieve and attach their tag.

8. The tagger must retreat from where the free pass is taken and then hand back the tag.

9. Free passes are awarded for infringements.

10. Infringements are: forward passing, knock-ons (Under 8s, not Under 7s), offside, diving to the ground, kicking, physical contact and the ball passing into touch. All result in a free pass.

11. Restarts after a try are taken with a free pass from the centre line by the non-scoring team.

3

EQUIPMENT, KIT AND PLAYERS

The equipment and kit needed for playing tag rugby are fairly simple. As no goals are scored, no posts are needed. Some teams will be lucky enough to have a tag rugby pitch that's marked out with white lines but this is not absolutely necessary. Marker cones are perfectly acceptable. In addition, you will need the correct size of rugby ball – a size 3 – for each game being played, but if you're doing exercises and drills you will need several balls.

In terms of kit, young players will need suitable long-sleeved sports shirts, shorts (or tracksuit bottoms in extremely cold weather), socks, rugby boots (or suitable sports shoes, depending on the surface being played on) and, of course, tags and tag belts. When setting up a team for the first time, and especially if there are financial constraints, it is not necessary for teams to have identical kit. As long as the tags are all the same colour for each team then the game of tag rugby can be played and enjoyed with otherwise unmatching attire. Obviously, when competing in leagues, competitions or tournaments, players should have matching kit displaying their team colours.

Very often, a committed parent or local business will sponsor your kit, which, in the case of the business at least, benefits them as much as your team because they will gain valuable advertising and publicity. This is why it can be very helpful to have someone in the club who deals specifically with raising money and sponsorship, leaving the coaches and referees to get on with the game. There is more information on this in Chapter 10 (see pages 157–163).

Equipment

- **One rugby ball** per game, size 3.

- **Cones** or similar to mark out the corners and centre line.

- **Tag belts** with a Velcro patch on either side for each player.

- **Two tags** with Velcro patches for each player.

Sports kit

Both boys and girls should wear the following:

- **sports shirts and shorts**, or tracksuits, with tops tucked in.

- **rugby boots or sports shoes**: if boots are worn, the teacher, coach or referee should check that they are approved by the IRB (International Rugby Board, the world governing and law-making body for rugby union). Wearing the right studs is very important; they should bear the kitemark. The wrong type of studs could result in injury either to the player wearing them, or to another player.

- **tag belts and tags**: the belts are worn around the waist with tags hanging down on either side of the hips. No part of the tag belt should flap when the belt has been secured around the waist – the ends should be tucked firmly out of the way. This is important to prevent injury to the players.

MATCHING STRIP

It's not necessary for clothing to match for school lessons or local community clubs but it is helpful if the team tags match. In competitions, each team wears its own colours.

- **mouthguards**: the RFU strongly recommends that mouthguards are worn for protection against collision with another player, or a fall. Preferably, these mouthguards should be made from an impression of the player's teeth by a dentist or dental technician. However, they can be very expensive and cannot be used second-hand, so a less expensive option is a do-it-yourself kit, available from most sports shops.

Tags and tag belts

Each player wears a belt that has two tags: one on either side of their waist. The tags are attached to the belt by Velcro and are easy to grab hold of. These tags are made of strips of strong material, natural or synthetic, which may be in a team's colours or carry the logo of a sponsor. Each team should have a different coloured tag from their opponents for easy identification.

Remember: only the tag may be pulled from an opponent's belt. Grabbing, pulling, or any physical contact with other player is not allowed and if it happens a penalty is awarded to the other side in the form of a free pass.

The rugby ball

Last but not least, as regards equipment, is the rugby ball itself. One of the best aspects of the senior game of rugby at any level is the shape of the ball because this makes play so unpredictable, especially when kicking is involved. In tag rugby there is no kicking of any kind so a fast-moving bouncing ball that's been kicked won't be a problem. However, the shape of the ball probably makes it easier to catch than a round ball.

EGG-SHAPED!

A weird shape or what, this oval ball? A rugby ball has four panels stitched together. In the past these were made of leather, making the ball quite heavy and prone to getting very wet and even heavier. Leather balls continued to be produced right up to the 1980s but by then synthetic materials began to be used. Today a rugby ball is made of hi-spec materials which don't get the ball so wet and help to keep its shape. A senior rugby ball is 280–300mm in length and weighs around 410–440g, although smaller balls are generally used for junior teams, and size 3 for minis.

Referees

It's obvious that referees should not wear the same strip as either of the teams playing but even if this does happen it's not a problem because the referee will be an adult, and will therefore stand well above the players. As for the players themselves, rugby boots and rugby shorts, shirts and socks are the kit and, of course, a whistle is essential. A notebook and pencil are needed to record the scores.

Duration of play

A match is made up of two halves, each of 10 minutes' duration, with a two-minute interval at half-time, although referees and coaches should tailor the game to suit the conditions, weather, and age of the players. If there is to be a change of playing duration then the coaches of both sides must be in agreement. It's not up to one side to set a different duration of play without consulting the opposing team.

Health and safety

It's a good idea for mini players to sit down at half-time, if it's not too cold or wet, and have a small snack such as fruit, maybe an orange segment, and a drink of water. Encourage parents not to give them chocolate bars and sweets to eat at half-time. These may lie heavy on their stomachs, and may also (along with fizzy drinks) hype up the players. Such food and drink can be eaten after the game. Absolutely no chewing gum, bubblegum or any other sweets or food should be in their mouths while playing the game, to ensure that there's no possibility of choking. That goes for the referees and coaches too, as they should be setting an example.

If an emergency should occur, referees and coaches should be familiar with first-aid procedures. Having a basic knowledge of first aid is essential and further courses at higher levels are advisable. Your local St John's Ambulance or local council will run first-aid courses.

Starting play

Play begins when the two teams have lined up across the width of the pitch in their own halves on either side of the centre line. Each team faces the other and the team who won the toss will begin with a free pass when the referee blows his or her whistle.

The full rules are in Chapter 2 (see pages 23–37).

Who can play?

Everybody! Girls and boys can play in mixed teams in their year groups in schools, or in a close mix of ages in clubs. Tag rugby will develop a varying range of skills and fitness levels but does not depend exclusively upon individuals who excel at sports, nor brute strength. The emphasis is on agile running and ball handling and there's a place for anyone who wants to play at whatever level of skill. Above all, tag rugby is not boring. It can be fast and exciting and will improve team spirit.

CHILDREN WITH LEARNING DIFFICULTIES AND THOSE WHO ARE DISABLED

If you have children in your school or club who have learning difficulties, or who are disabled, there is no reason why they shouldn't play tag rugby. In fact, the Disability Discrimination Acts of 1995 and 2005 (DDA 1995 and DDA 2005) make it illegal to exclude children with a disability from such activities. The DDAs aren't there to make your life more difficult but to make the lives of disabled children easier and more inclusive.

If you have a child with Down's Syndrome there is no reason why they shouldn't be encouraged to play. It may be that catching and passing are difficult to master, but bear in mind that a child doesn't have to be disabled to have poor hand/eye coordination. Be mindful too, that not all disabled children have the same levels of disability so you'll need to assess the child's capabilities and allow play accordingly. Thankfully, tag rugby is a very simple game and most children should be able to grasp the simple concepts of the game and to achieve the skills necessary to be part of a team.

Problems?

If there are problems, with a child who is overweight, very tall or very small for their age you can make allowances in all sorts of ways, but remember that an unusual physique doesn't necessarily lead to a disadvantage. Initially a child should be encouraged to play normally with the team that matches their age group, and then you will be in a better position to assess whether they need further help. It's best practice to keep an eye on all the players anyway and assess their progress and act accordingly.

If you have a physically disabled child who is interested in tag rugby, you will need to consult with the parents or carers about the level of involvement in this sport which they think is suitable for their child. The child should also have a say in what they feel they can do, and then all parties concerned can decide whether it is possible for that child to play. Even if it's not practical for them to play, there are lots of things that children can do to be part of the team that don't involve passing the ball and scoring tries.

A struggling child?

If you notice that any child, whether they are disabled or not, is really struggling and becoming disheartened then discuss this with the child to see if you can pinpoint the problem. It may be a lack of confidence, or that no one ever passes the ball to them, or other such reasons, which can be easily overcome if referees and coaches are aware of them, but there may be other, more serious reasons not connected with rugby. This is a complicated issue that is not always easy to identify and can be easy to get wrong. In Chapter 9 (see pages 147–155) you will find further essential information about this.

If it's simply a matter of lacking in confidence or skill, ask the child if she or he would like to continue running with the ball until two tags have been removed instead of one. The tagger only shouts 'Tag!' when the second tag is taken, so it will give the player extra time and space to make their run. Or it may be that no one is passing the ball to them. Find out why and encourage the others to include this child in their play. Don't accept the argument that this player always gets tagged so there's no point in passing the ball to them. Explain that no one will improve their game if they never get the ball and that in order to develop as players, they need to learn from other players who may be of a different level to them. Remind your team to be good sports and play together as a team.

If you decide that a special course of action should be taken for a particular child, then talk to the others in the team and get them to understand that this isn't favouritism or giving an unfair advantage. Explain how the problem can be solved with their help and cooperation but do not discuss confidential personal affairs about that child with any other players or parents/carers. You can explain to them that special measures will help the player become more skilled and move up to the other players' level if given the chance.

Obviously, it will be difficult to change the rules at competition level but, like the Paralympics, it is possible to arrange for less skilled or disabled teams to play and compete at their own level.

Wheelchairs or other mobility restrictions

If there is a child who uses a wheelchair, or is unable to take part for some other medical reason, you can still involve them in the game. Ask her or him to be a touch judge on the

> ### TASKS FOR NON-PLAYERS
> There are lots of tasks that non-players can do such as keeping the score, handing out and collecting tags, being near the try line to ensure that tries are scored correctly or giving calls. They can also help the coach to give advice at half-time and the end of the game. Inclusion in whatever capacity is the key.

goal line to make sure that the ball is grounded properly. You can also get them to keep a record of the score in a notebook. If you are refereeing you will, of course, need to keep a record of the score yourself but you can compare notes with your touch judge during the match and at half and full time. (See Chapter 8, pages 137–145 for more on refereeing.)

Many disabled children, even those who need wheelchairs, attend their local school and are included in the sports activities there, so there is no reason why sports clubs can't do the same. In the Paralympics there are the notorious wheelchair teams competing in rugby and the sport's nickname isn't 'Murderball' for nothing. Essentially a kind of tag rugby, except the 'tagging' in this version is to hit another player with the ball, taking them out of the game, so their aim is to avoid being tagged. In view of this, it's easy to see why so many collisions and crashes occur. The last man sitting is the winner. It's fascinating to watch but not a gentle game. The wheelchair players certainly take no prisoners! Obviously, I don't advocate such a strong approach to the game for minis, but it shows that everyone can have a go at this sport in whatever form.

> **PARALYMPICS**
>
> The 2012 Paralympics held in London was a triumph for disabled athletes and was as popular for spectators as the Olympics. Competitors such as Ellie Simmonds OBE, who has a height of 1.23m, captured the hearts of a nation when she won two gold medals, plus a silver and a bronze, for swimming. An example to everyone!

Involve them

Above all, don't be frightened of disabled children involving themselves in sport, particularly tag rugby. My eldest son has epilepsy and has played rugby at senior level as a flanker and on the wing. He wore headgear to protect himself but this didn't always prevent a seizure. If he was playing rugby and realised that he was about to have a seizure he notified the nearest players and took himself to the sideline for safety. His team-mates were aware of his condition and knew what to do to ensure that he didn't harm himself. Needless to say, he didn't continue to play the rest of that match but he was back in the next game as soon as possible after his recovery!

4 COACHING

Before you begin

Take a look at Chapter 9 (see pages 147–155), which deals with the safeguarding of children. This is *essential* reading or revision before you undertake any kind of work with children in the world of rugby and you will need to be DBS (Disclosure and Barring Service) checked. This is a check of police records to make sure that you haven't got any convictions or cautions regarding inappropriate behaviour towards children. Children need to be protected from abuse of any kind and in whatever form, physical or sexual, and you and your club have a statutory duty to ensure that those in your club or school are safe to work with children. Don't worry if you got into trouble as a teenager through hijinks and got involved with the police. This won't prevent you from being a rugby coach. As long as you're a trustworthy and respected person in adult life you can leave your adolescent days behind. Likewise, your sexuality will be no barrier to being a coach.

All coaches and referees will need to ensure that they aren't alone with children or particularly a single child. Always be with another adult in changing rooms. Having another adult present is a real safeguard. It's common sense and will protect you from accusation that results from misunderstanding or malicious intent.

Even if as a coach or referee you think you know everything about the game, it is advisable to check again and remind yourself of the rules. They do change from time to time and the most important aspect of your coaching and training has to be the well-being of the children in your care. However, don't be too complacent or naive. You may not be a bully or abuser yourself, nor running a club badly, but others may be and it is your duty to look out for this and any other problems with the children in your care. If you suspect something is amiss, make a record of your concerns and then contact the appropriate authority to report it. All the details and information you need for this are covered in Chapter 9.

However, don't be put off by all these safeguards and requirements. It's all common sense really, but today we are more aware of how children can be maltreated and the children themselves are, quite rightly, aware of their rights and more protected by law than they were in the past. Knowing the guidelines and understanding where to draw the line will protect you and all in your care.

DO THE RIGHT THING

Any sport can have coaches who are bullies or child abusers somewhere in its ranks, so those involved in rugby must not become complacent and think that it could never happen in our sport. Be vigilant. If you suspect something is wrong, take action. It's better to do something for the right intentions and be mistaken than to do nothing at all.

Safety first

If you are coaching children, you should not only have a well-equipped first-aid kit handy, but should also have good first-aid knowledge, preferably having attended a course run by the St John Ambulance, your local council or a similar organisation. Don't be fooled into thinking, 'It's only a few kids running around, so where's the harm in that?' The fact is that an injury can happen at any time and can often be caused by something that may appear perfectly innocuous. A player can run into another player, catch an elbow in the face, roll over on an ankle or slip and fall, and while this may not necessarily lead to an injury, it could do – so be prepared. Very young players don't have the muscle development to withstand heavy knocks to their bodies so it may seem as though they're being 'babies' if they cry when they fall down, but remember how young they are and be kind and understanding. Don't indulge them but don't be too harsh either. Shouting at them to get up and stop being a wimp isn't called for. Ask them if they're OK and, if they are, try to get them back on their feet and into the game as soon as possible. Little ones are distracted very easily so they'll soon forget that they had a fall.

You will need to know, however, if there are children in the group with pre-existing medical conditions, and you'll need to know what to do if a player has an epileptic seizure or goes into anaphylactic shock. Encourage the children and their parent or carers to let you know of any potential medical problems. This will help you to plan your coaching or teaching sessions more effectively and safely. Remember about data protection though, and be careful with how you keep records and who you tell.

Already had some experience?

Excellent. The club needs you but make sure you really know the rules of the game as set out in Chapter 2 (see pages 23–37). Get someone to test you, or test yourself.

New to all this?

Where do you start out as a coach? If you're a PE teacher you will have the advantage of ready-made facilities and captive players so you won't need to look for venues and basic equipment. However, all coaches and teachers will need to acquire coaching skills, learn the RFU's Rules of Tag Rugby and practise being a good coach. Familiarise yourself with the coaching methods in this chapter, the exercises and drills in Chapter 5, the games in Chapter 6, and the lesson plans in Chapter 7, then go for it!

Starting up a club or team

First of all, you will need to find out where you can practise and improve your coaching skills. You may be able to join a tag rugby club either at a school or at community club level.

However, there are still lots of schools and places where tag rugby is not played. Rugby is such a great family sport that this is a real pity. If this is the case in your school or neighbourhood, why not start up a tag rugby team? Through tag and mini rugby you can bring on your youngest players to junior and then senior rugby – and perhaps even to academy status. This will help to nurture the professional rugby stars of the future. Mike Brown, English international and Harlequins player, started off playing rugby as a boy at club level and went on to become a professional at the top via the Harlequins Academy. Wouldn't it be great to know that you originally coached the next Mike Brown as a mini player? However, it's not just about working towards stardom. Tag rugby is fun to play and, judging from the games that go on every week all over the country and the many competitions and tournaments, it's a great family day out with the opportunity to watch a professional match and see some real international stars playing for their clubs.

If you want to start up a club of your own in the community from scratch, or if you want your club to join in such activities, contact your nearest senior club or the RFU. The RFU is a generous and committed supporter of community rugby and should be your first port of call for advice on both theoretical and practical tag rugby. Their website is www.rfu.co.uk, where you will find a wealth of information. You can also find the details of schools in your area from your local telephone directory and on your local council's website if they have a sports and leisure page.

For more information on running your own club visit the RFU site, find Managing Rugby and click on Developing Your Community Rugby, where there is a lot of information. Clubs should also contact the Rugby Development Officer (RDO) at the RFU who will give advice to clubs and schools.

WHAT'S IT LIKE TO BE A CLUB COACH?

Jon Burton was Head Coach for tag rugby for some years at Salisbury RFC. For Jon, coaching is about leadership, inspiring young people to excel and, above all, making the game great fun for the players. This is exactly what the RFU wants to see at community level. Rugby teaches fellowship, team spirit, and acceptance of the word of the coach and referee.

This last point is important because dissent has no part in the game. Losing your temper or complaining that the refereeing isn't fair is to be thoroughly discouraged. I think it's fantastic that in the professional game of rugby if a player questions or makes rude remarks about a referee's decision then the referee will punish this swiftly and decisively. The offending player may be sin-binned for ten minutes or even sent off, and a penalty will be awarded to the opposing side. If the referee has already awarded a penalty before this offence took place he might move the spot where the penalty is to be taken 10m further on towards the opponent's try line. This could result in a kick at goal rather than a kick into touch for a line-out. It's a three-point give-away. It's a very good deterrent and ensures respect for referees. The other aspect of refereeing in the senior game is that the referee will call over the captain and the offending player and will speak to the captain about the infringement, leaving the captain to speak to his own player about the matter afterwards. It instils real respect for the referee and quashes any dissent right from the beginning.

PROGRESS AND ACHIEVEMENT

Coaches need a keen eye to spot those players who are beginning to struggle and those doing exceptionally well, and all the others in between. It's always gratifying when a player moves up to a higher team but there will be those who find they can't master the required skills quite so well. Know who they are and give them extra encouragement and even extra coaching, if necessary. A child who isn't enjoying the game or feels they're no good at it and that nobody cares will eventually stop coming to tag rugby.

Jon himself likes to be on the field refereeing during matches and truly loves to coach the Under 7s, but he stresses that we should all remind ourselves that it isn't always easy coaching very young children. We might be tempted to think that because they're so young there won't be any problems but the children's lack of maturity will make great demands on not only your patience, but also on your ability to keep their attention and on their understanding of the game. They have their own characters and need sympathetic understanding if you consider them to be awkward, cheeky or disruptive.

A PLACE FOR EVERY CHILD

Not every child is a natural at sports but there is a place for them. Let them know that and welcome them.

However, there's nothing Jon dislikes about coaching Under 7s. The weather doesn't bother him, although during really cold weather the club spends a lot of time keeping the children warm. It's the families watching from the sidelines who are the ones freezing! Also, bear in mind that the occasional parent will complain if they feel their child should be in a higher team, but Jon firmly but gently explains that he's the boss and makes the decisions. His long experience of club and competition tag rugby enables him to pick the best players for competitive teams but this shouldn't mean that the others are sidelined. Everyone likes to win, and so does Jon, but being part of the team is more important.

Many will achieve better skills in time and some will eventually go on to be in teams that play other clubs. And if they don't it doesn't matter. Don't be so ambitious for your child that nothing but being in the best team and being the best player will do. This is appalling pressure for a young child, regardless of whether they're your child or not. If they have the talent to do higher things it will show. If they haven't but they enjoy the game, then tag rugby has achieved its highest aim.

Being part of a club is a great experience. Clubs may put on free meals for visiting teams and have plenty of events, in addition to leagues and competitions, taking place throughout the season to keep everybody's interest. These could include race nights, discos, hosting a local tournament, the Mini Tour at the end of the season, and all sorts of entertainment for children and the adults. These events will also raise money for the club and ensure that the parents and carers meet one another and the children get together – usually outside to let off steam!

WHY COACH?

Think carefully about why you want to be a coach. Are you prepared to do for others more than they do for you, to learn, to be patient, to lead, to inspire, and to motivate very young players in the game? If you do, don't hesitate. Find a club, become a tag rugby coach – and have a great time!

WHAT TO DO IF YOU WANT TO COACH

Once you've decided you want to become a tag rugby coach you will need to complete a training course. The Start Coaching Tag Rugby course (see the RFU website) lasts for approximately three hours and is practical-based. There is no formal assessment, and the course is delivered by an accredited coach educator and is accompanied by a supporting DVD. At the conclusion of the course you will have gained:

- an understanding of how to deliver a safe and enjoyable practical session.

- knowledge of how to coach and improve skills through games.

- an understanding of the application of a game-sense approach.

- knowledge of the rules of tag rugby.

- the ability to apply of the rules of tag rugby (refereeing).

STARTING FROM SCRATCH

If you are starting from scratch, you will need to look around for a suitable place to train your teams and play your matches. There are always plenty of public areas or senior pitches and clubs that will be willing to play host to tag rugby enthusiasts. You may even be able to use a local school's facilities. You can probably find all the information you need from the internet, your local library, council, newspaper and magazines or advertising cards in newsagents' windows for venues for your club. If this fails, place an advertisement of your own for somewhere to train.

If it has not already been done, be prepared to have a DBS check. This is legally required if you are going to work with children.

BASIC EQUIPMENT

Once you've got your venue you will need the basic equipment: size 3 rugby balls, tags, tag belts, cones or markers for the pitch, a whistle if you wish and, of course, some players. All of you will need suitable sports clothing and sports shoes, or approved rugby boots, and the players will need mouthguards. Chapter 3 (see pages 39–47) has all the information on this.

Sports kit doesn't have to be fancy and matching when you start out, but if you need help with providing kit there are many different ways of raising funds. Have a look at Chapter 10 (see pages 157–163) for ideas on how to finance your club, beyond the subs you will need to charge your players each season to cover costs.

HELP WITH COACHING

It is always advisable to have at least one other adult or responsible older child with you, but having as many people as you can muster to help you will be a tremendous advantage. Having plenty of assistants will allow you to divide up the players into smaller groups and manage teams during a match. It is also a recommended safeguard in case of injury or accusation.

Adult parents or carers are usually the best bet. Some may be in a position to sponsor your club or school, so get them on your side. I've heard of dads who have sponsored the sports kit and even financed floodlighting. Also, some parents help out with refereeing teams on the field as well as the coaches. Make sure they know the rules. Then the referee will have an easier job.

COACHING IN A NUTSHELL

- Familiarise yourself with the ways to safeguard children in Chapter 9.

- Find a suitable place to coach and play.

- Make sure you know the rules of tag rugby (see Chapter 2).

- Be familiar with how to coach and know the exercises, drills and games. Look at the RFU's website for initial help.

- Find enough players.

- Ensure you have the necessary equipment and sports clothing.

- Have fellow coaches or other adults to help you.

- Know your first aid and have a first-aid kit handy.

- Finally, enjoy it!

Community rugby

Community rugby refers to all the clubs and schools at grass roots level that are so important in keeping the game going and sparking the interest that will lead to years of supporting rugby. As stated, at the very beginning is tag rugby. Go along to your local club and join in.

JOIN IN WITH THE PROFESSIONALS TOO

Most of the professional clubs throughout the divisions encourage junior rugby, including tag rugby, and have supported community rugby for years. They encourage clubs and schools to become associates and make use of the facilities and events they offer through their community teams. It is in their interests to foster and develop rugby at all levels and tag rugby is where it usually begins for very young children.

With links to local schools and clubs, sometimes as many as 80 or more, your school or club could be part of this. Of course, it's in the professional club's interests to promote rugby union and tie in supporters, but they are genuinely interested in promoting the game at community level so it's up to you to take advantage of this. As an associate your club will have access to managers and coaches who are employed specifically to help.

On match day there will often be tag, mini, and youth teams competing before the main match so it's a great opportunity not only to show off your team's skills but also to play against lots of other clubs and to see a professional match afterwards. It's a delight to see the visiting tag rugby teams playing on the main pitch during half-time. Some of the tag rugby players are tiny but they are just as determined as the older ones to play well and win. Families come to support their children and watch the professionals slugging it out.

Tag teams will usually form part of the guard of honour along with the other junior players at the start of the big match with a club flag. They politely cheer the visiting team as they run out onto the pitch but then they erupt into even louder cheering and flag-waving when the home side run out. It's quite magical for them because these young players are very close to some of the biggest names in rugby who play for their country, as well as international players from all over the world, including France, Italy, Australia, New Zealand, South Africa and the Pacific islands.

Tag rugby players can also get the chance to be a mascot for a match, run out onto the pitch with the team captain and have their photo taken. For details of how to become a mascot look in the match programme of your club or on the team's website.

MAKE EXTRA MONEY FOR YOUR CLUB

Some professional clubs run a cash-back system that enables clubs to buy ten match-day tickets at a discount, say, ten for the price of seven. This means that a club can sell their tickets at the full price and raise money for their club.

Find out where your nearest professional club is by looking on the RFU website. Your local club may run all sorts of activities, including community rugby and tag rugby competitions, which you can take part in.

FIND SPONSORSHIP

One of the best ways to ensure that your club succeeds and flourishes is to find sponsorship. Most community programmes would not take place without it. Sponsorship enables a very full season of competition and support. See Chapter 10 (see pages 157–163) for further ideas about funding your club.

If they don't, why not have a go at persuading them? It will benefit them as much as it will you and your tag rugby team or club.

Maintaining discipline

When working with children it is essential to maintain discipline, earn their respect and not be too friendly, or they will take advantage of you and you may find yourself open to criticism or accusation. However, being too hard-line won't work either. Overenthusiastic encouragement of your team to excel and win can lead to bullying the players. Don't let this happen to you. Maintaining discipline with children is always a delicate balance between keeping order and not being too regimented or too friendly.

Keeping order is very important because ultimately the safety of all the children in your care depends on it. Also, in an orderly environment children are less likely to be bullied by their peers and much more likely to enjoy themselves. Encourage your players to say something nice, to look for the positive, or not say anything at all. You may think that calling a child names like 'fatso' or 'shorty' is harmless fun or will toughen them up, but such remarks can be deeply wounding. They are not appropriate and can undermine and upset a child who is sensitive about him/herself.

BE SYMPATHETIC

If you feel a child is overweight, don't single him or her out with comments or actions. You may be able to help with a general emphasis on fitness and the desirability to eat healthily by speaking to all the children about fitness, but remember that young children have very little influence over how their lives are run. You may be able to discourage them from bringing unsuitable snacks and drinks to your coaching sessions, but you cannot lay down rules for what happens at home. You can, however, give a talk to the parents and carers about the relationship between a healthy diet and being fit so that they are aware of its importance. Gaining their cooperation is key to ensuring that the children in your care achieve fitness, not only through exercise but also through a healthy lifestyle.

BE FIRM BUT NOT HARSH

You can often defuse a potentially bad-tempered situation with a bit of humour. If the players see you as grumpy and miserable, they won't cooperate. If the adults think you're a tyrant, you'll lose their goodwill too.

Once you have established a really good relationship with the teams you are coaching you will be able to have a joke and engage in friendly banter and no one will be offended. It will also encourage the children not to take you, themselves, or the game too seriously.

TAKING CARE

Don't expect to like all children

Children are the same as adults as regards their characters: they can be easy-going, shy, cheeky, bombastic, know-it-all, kind, unkind, caring and so on. Some you will naturally take to more than others but you should try not to let this influence either the way you treat each child or the decisions you make. Children have an innate sense of fairness and will immediately spot favouritism or bias, but remember that they'll probably still grumble, however fair you are! See the Codes of Conduct in the appendix at the back of this book. They are based on the RFU's codes and will help to ensure that you and your club maintain the high level of behaviour that is expected in rugby.

Parent power

Parents will have their opinions about who you choose for the team, especially if you haven't chosen their child. Parent pester power pops up everywhere and can be a real nuisance, but you are in charge so don't be defensive. Explain the reason for your choice and stick to it. If you have too many players for a team, you can rotate them and give each child a chance of playing. However, if you know you are doing the right thing you will have to learn to live with not being popular with all of the parents all of the time.

Be firm about not tolerating interference or too much vocal encouragement from the adults on the sidelines and under no circumstances tolerate bad or abusive language of any nature from anybody, adults or players. People can get carried away with their passion; that's understandable. Children will naturally be ecstatic when they win, especially if it's a trophy in a tournament, but triumphalism and disrespect for the losing side must never be tolerated. Lack of respect, anger and intolerance or baiting other players all contribute towards an aggressive attitude that at its worst can spill over into violence. So nip it in the bud and encourage a good sporting attitude that will allow enthusiasm and cheering for a child or team, but not at the expense of a pleasant and safe atmosphere.

GOOD CONDUCT CODES

Give parents and carers a copy of the Good Parent's Code, which is printed in the appendix of this book and based on the RFU's recommendations. So far, rugby at all levels has remained largely unblemished by organised hooliganism among its supporters and, thankfully, so far there is no need for supporters of different teams to be in separate sections of the stadium at matches, nor for the supporters to be segregated and escorted to and from the match by the police. Despite all the fierce rivalry, and especially at the big internationals, you mix with the other supporters and congratulate the winners or commiserate with the losers after the match. Yes, you'll feel elated and want to shout a bit but remember also to play your part in keeping rugby free from unpleasantness. No abuse of other supporters, no nasty baiting them, no inflammatory remarks. After all, it's only a game.

BE PEACEFUL AND POLITE

At the end of a Six Nations match between England and Scotland at Twickenham, I stopped to pat a police horse and was surprised to see that neither horse nor rider were wearing any protective gear. There were no shin guards or blinkers for the horse, and no face guard or riot shield for the policewoman. When I expressed my surprise at this, she explained that at rugby matches it wasn't necessary because the supporters were peaceful and polite. That's fantastic. Let's all keep it this way!

A FEW PRINCIPLES

It can be very daunting to have a group of children to organise and coach effectively and safely for an hour or more. So remember a few principles:

- **You're in charge**. Make sure all the children are attentive and listen when you wish to speak to them. If you stand still and quietly yourself once you've called for them to be quiet, it will soon dawn on the chatterboxes that you are waiting. Do this for as long as it takes, but then tell the children that if they continue to talk when you've called for quiet you will apply a sanction.

- **Let them know what you expect of them** – no bullying and so on – and tell them that self-discipline is very important for sport in terms of safety, courtesy, improvement and enjoyment.

- **Don't tolerate petty tale-telling** but do let them know that if they have a genuine problem of any sort they should come and tell you in confidence, especially if it concerns bullying.

- Have a strategy for dealing with **bullying** of any kind – whether physical, racist or sexist in nature.

HOW TO TACKLE BULLYING

First and foremost, it essential that coaches and referees aren't bullies themselves. It's always a good idea to review your own attitudes and behaviour. If you lose your temper quickly, if you are easily irritated, and if you tend to shout or speak out regardless, now is the time to think about how you can overcome this because working with such young children calls for immense patience and tolerance. (See also Chapter 9.)

As for the players, encourage the children in your care to tell you if they are being bullied, and look out for it yourself. Be firm initially. Make it very clear that you will not tolerate such poor behaviour, but also try to understand why it is happening. Bullies have sometimes been bullied themselves and usually have a problem with self-image, so try to praise them and build up their confidence so they don't need to pick on others. Foster a good team spirit and encourage the children to help others in the team. Talk to all the children about this problem and get them on your side. It's cool to care.

Before the coaching session

PERSONAL SAFETY

Check the following as regards the players before you start each coaching session.

- No child should be wearing jewellery that is likely to cause injury to him/herself or to another child.

- Check footwear and clothing: are they suitable for your pitch conditions and the session itself?

- Long hair: is it tied back securely?

- Encourage all players to wear mouthguards. They don't just protect teeth, they also protect the tongue, jaw and skull.

- Have plenty of drinking water ready for half-time. If children are allowed their own drinks, try to encourage them to choose sports drinks that contain the necessary carbohydrates (like sucrose and glucose) and electrolytes (sodium and potassium). These prevent dehydration and provide extra energy. They are more effective but also more expensive than water.

- Healthy snacks: encourage the children to go for energy bars or cereal bars rather than crisps and chocolate containing colouring and additives, which may hype them up in the wrong way. If cereal bars are too expensive and you have a child or adult who loves cooking and has the time, you could ask them to make some flapjacks or similar cakes packed with energy and goodness.

SAFETY OF THE GROUND AND SURROUNDINGS

Check the following before every session.

- Hazards such as glass or solid walls. Have a pair of heavy-duty gardening gloves and a strong bag handy for picking up any broken glass or drinks cans. Note whether there are any walls or fences close to play.

- Animal waste. This may be from dogs or foxes. While it is a legal requirement now to pick up after your dog, not all dog owners scoop, so if you're playing on a public ground a good search of the playing area is advisable.

- Markings: are they clear and correct?

How to plan a coaching session

Running straight out on to a field to play a game of tag rugby is neither advisable from an exercise point of view or for sports safety, nor is it going to help improve your players' skills. A gradual build-up to a vigorous game of rugby will get the maximum out of your coaching session and will contribute to an enjoyable experience for the players. One way of planning a coaching session is as follows:

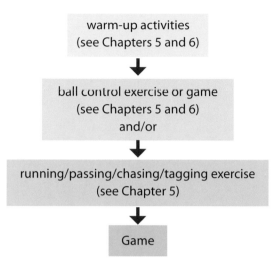

Use the lesson plans in Chapter 7 to start off and establish a routine. Whatever you're doing, don't forget to keep fun and enjoyment as top priorities for the young players. The more they enjoy your sessions, the more they'll cooperate with what you're trying to achieve, and the more you motivate them, the better they'll play. This way everyone wins!

Remember that there are always marked physical differences in size, weight and height between children of the same age at junior school, so be prepared for this. Try to balance the difference in your teams and ensure that you pitch your exercises and drills at the correct level for the age of the children you're coaching and their experience of playing tag rugby. The lesson plans in Chapter 7 are graded and include exercises and games. They start with sessions for absolute beginners who have never played tag rugby before, while the last sessions consolidate what has been learned so that the players are prepared for a full game of tag rugby.

AFTER THE MATCH OR COACHING SESSION

After the match or coaching session, the children should perform some warm-down exercises (see Chapter 5). Afterwards, gather the players around and speak positively about the session. This will ensure a good sporting attitude and team spirit.

BE POSITIVE!

Always praise the positive aspects of the game and let the players know that you will be practising any aspect of their play that needs improvement.

FELLOWSHIP AND TEAM SPIRIT

Have a drink together to rehydrate your body after vigorous exercise. Smoothies and yoghurts are excellent for replacing energy as the protein and carbohydrates in them will help glycogen recovery, but there's nothing wrong with a good drink of water. This also encourages a sense of being part of a team off the field. If everyone runs off and goes home straight after the game or session, you lose that sense of club togetherness.

Finally, be prepared to enjoy what you're doing and make it exciting for the players too!

NEGATIVE CAN BE POSITIVE

As a coach or teacher you will need to point out where improvements in team play and individual skills are needed, but this doesn't have to be a negative experience. 'A fantastic effort team, but next time we're going to see if we can win, aren't we?' 'That was good running, Peter, but don't forget to find space and sidestep to avoid being tagged.' 'You tried really hard at tagging, Clare, and we'll all be able to have more practice at this in the next session.'

Take a look at the RFU Fair Play Codes in the appendix. They will help you, the players, assistants, spectators and match officials to participate in and observe the game in a spirit of understanding, positive encouragement, enjoyment and appreciation.

FINALLY: BE PASSIONATE!

To be a coach you have to be really passionate about the game and love working with children. It can be demanding and time-consuming, but it is always very rewarding and enjoyable.

5 EXERCISES AND DRILLS

You can combine the exercises and drills in this chapter with the fun and games in Chapter 6 to make your own coaching sessions. Alternatively, you can use the lesson and coaching plans in Chapter 7.

Warming up/warming down

Why? Warming-up exercises are important in any sport for three reasons:

- **Practical** – Learning or practising skills. These exercises develop the basic skills needed to play tag rugby and will improve play.

- **Physical** – warming up gently stretches muscles, aids mobility, increases flow of blood to muscles and helps prevent injury.

- **Psychological** – a good warm-up prepares players mentally for tasks ahead, improves concentration and encourages team spirit.

Warming down after a session lets the players recover from vigorous exercise:

- **Physical** – allows the body to return to normal resting state.

- **Psychological** – mentally calms the players down.

TIPS FOR WARMING-UP AND WARMING-DOWN EXERCISES

- It is important, particularly if the players are new to tag rugby, for them to hold a ball in both hands for these exercises so that they can practise running with the ball.

- Give clear instructions and demonstrations and ensure that they all understand what to do.

- Ensure that the players get moving quickly and don't get cold or bored.

- Keep an eye on all the players and help out any group which is struggling.

- When suitable, introduce competition between teams or individuals to create an element of fun and interest.

At the start

Begin gently or there is the risk of muscle strain. The whole object of warming up is to prepare the body for sustained energetic exercise, so the players need to work up to this in a **controlled way**. Mix exercises at a gentle jogging pace with those that can be done standing still.

When they're warmed up you can play any of the games in Chapter 6 or organise matches among the players.

These exercises can be done by **beginners or more experienced** players because there are easy and advanced levels of each exercise to choose from.

OUTSIDE/INSIDE

All exercises and games are for outdoor activity but if the weather is bad they can be just as effective indoors if there is enough space in a sports hall or club building.

Equipment needed for exercises and drills

● One ball for each team of players.

● At least 24 markers.

● Bib or bands for half the players if they are wearing the same strip.

● One tag belt with two affixed tags per player.

NOT ENOUGH CONES?

If you don't have enough cones ask the children to make markers for you with large cardboard circles of about one metre in diameter and to colour them in bright colours. These markers will be just as effective as cones and much cheaper.

MARKING OUT THE PITCH

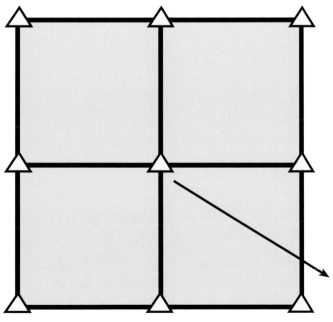

Grid layout

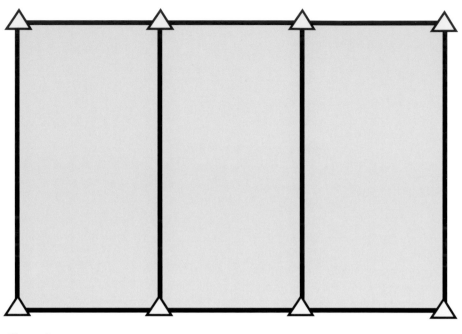

Channels

GRIDS AND CHANNELS

● Use lines and/or markers on the playing surface.

● The size of the grids should reflect the age and ability of the players, and the type of activity being performed.

● For very young players grids of 10m × 10m are sufficient.

● Several grids can be joined to make larger areas by the removal of the central marker, which ensures quick movement throughout the session.

● Channels are formed by marking out a series of rectangles on the pitch. They are particularly good for practising passing and in groups.

MARK THEM CLEARLY

If you can, use different coloured markers for each grid or channel. This will help the players to see the boundaries for their playing area.

1. Touch ball

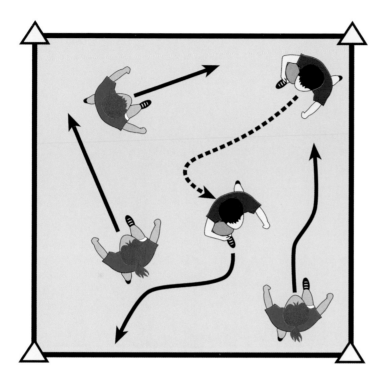

AIMS

- To develop running and evasion skills.

PLAYERS/EQUIPMENT

- Grids 20m × 20m marked out by cones or markers.

- Groups of 5.

- 1 × size 3 ball per team.

HOW TO PLAY

- The ball carrier tries to touch as many players as possible with the ball.

- The other players look for space to run into and should not be within 1m of the other runners.

- The ball carrier keeps count of the number of times players are touched with the ball.

- After one minute, the teacher or coach calls 'Stop!' and the ball is handed over to another player.

DISABLED CHILDREN

If a child has very reduced mobility or is in a wheelchair then she/he can record who has received a touch ball and how often. Once a player has been touched by the ball she/he has to report this to the disabled child. At the end of the game the players will know how successful they have been in this exercise.

COACHING TIPS

- Ball carrier must keep both hands on the ball at all times and touch other players very gently.

- Encourage the players to look for space.

- Remind them of the evasion rule, and to dodge other players.

VARIATIONS

Easy

Reduce the dimensions of the grid.

Advanced

Increase the dimensions of the grid and/or add a rule that the touched player must be touched twice before the ball carrier moves on to another player.

2. Crossing the channel (teams of 4)

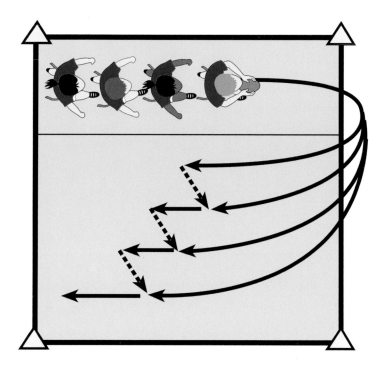

AIMS

● To develop running and passing skills and to work as a team to find space.

PLAYERS/EQUIPMENT

● Two channels – one 20m × 15m and one 20m × 5m.

● Teams of 4 players, one of whom is the ball carrier.

● Size 3 rugby ball per group.

HOW TO PLAY

● The first team lines up behind the ball carrier at one end of the narrow channel.

● They run to the other end of the narrow channel then turn into the wide channel and fan out.

- The ball carrier passes to the player next to him/her and so on along the line.

- As one team turns into the wide channel the next team sets off.

DISABLED CHILDREN

If a child has very reduced mobility or is in a wheelchair then he/she can give the call for each team to start when the team in front has turned into the wide channel and the ball has been passed at least twice. This will allow the coach to concentrate on skills development.

COACHING TIPS

- In the narrow channel the ball carrier should be told to get ahead so that he/she can change direction and slow down before delivering a pass.

- The others in the team should be told to try to keep within easy passing range of the ball carrier once they are in the wide channel.

- Encourage the ball carrier to look ahead when running but look at the other player's position and hands when passing.

VARIATIONS

Easy

The players start with a run until they reach the wide channel when they can slow down to a jog or even a walk if they are beginners.

Advanced

Add another defender or even two to make teams of 5 or 6.

3. Conga (teams of 5)

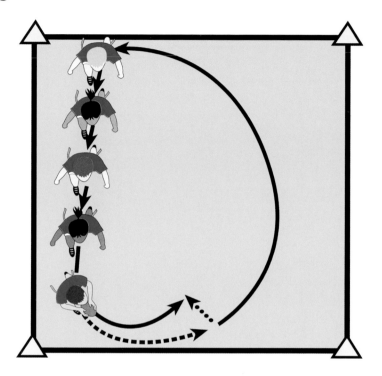

AIMS

- Developing skills for passing and support.

PLAYERS/EQUIPMENT

- Grids 20m × 20m.

- Teams of 5 players.

- One size 3 rugby ball per group.

HOW TO PLAY

- The ball carrier is the leader.

- The other players form a line behind.

- The ball carrier can run in any direction and the rest must follow.

- When the coach or teacher calls 'Pass!' the ball carrier must stop and hold out the ball to one side.

- The next player in line takes the ball and continues running in any direction as the new leader.

- The former ball carrier joins the back of the team.

DISABLED CHILDREN

If a child has very reduced mobility or is in a wheelchair then he/she can give the call for the ball carrier to 'Pass!' He/she could also call 'Change!' which would mean the ball carrier must change direction. This will allow the coach to concentrate on skills development.

COACHING TIPS

Encourage the players to:

- Run into space.

- Follow the ball carrier.

- Leave a good space between players.

- Try to take the ball without slowing down.

VARIATIONS

Easy

Walk or jog.

Advanced

Change the method of passing the ball such as placing the ball on the ground with both hands. It should be picked up with both hands. Or it could be passed in the normal way. These two methods could be sequential with the call 'Ground!' and then 'Pass two hands!' and then 'Ground!' and so on.

4. Calling the shots (teams of 4)

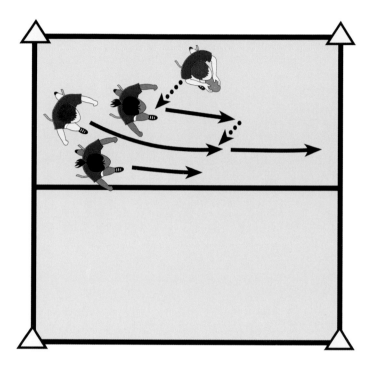

AIMS

- To develop running and passing skills and to work as a team.

PLAYERS/EQUIPMENT

- Two adjacent channels of equal size – 20m × 10m.

- Teams of 4 players.

- Size 3 rugby ball per team.

HOW TO PLAY

- Three players fan out away from the ball carrier and run through the channel.

- The last player in the team is the fourth player and receives the ball.

- The ball carrier must get her/himself in a position to pass, level or ahead of the other players.

- The ball carrier calls 'Pass!'

- The fourth player bursts through and gets into a position to receive the pass and calls for the pass.

- The team then runs on to the next channel repeating this action.

DISABLED CHILDREN

If a child has very reduced mobility or is in a wheelchair then he/she can give the call for each group to start when the group in front has turned into the wide channel and the ball has been passed again. This will allow the coach to concentrate on skills development.

COACHING TIPS

Encourage the players to:

- Space out, not bunch together.

- Listen to the call of the ball carrier for the pass.

- As the fourth player, find space and let team-mates know she/he is ready to burst through.

- Achieve explosive pace through the line of the team-mates.

- As the ball carrier, get into a position close to receiver.

VARIATIONS

Easy

The first attackers walk or jog slowly while the fourth player can run once the call for the pass has been given.

Advanced

Add a defender who will try to tag.

5. It's a try! (teams of 5)

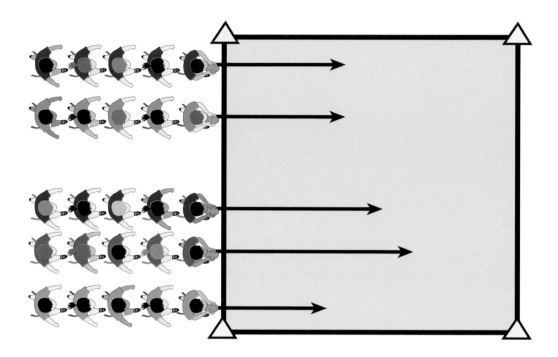

AIMS

- To develop individual ball skills in relays.

PLAYERS/EQUIPMENT

- Mark out a line 10m from the start line.

- Teams of 5.

- One size 3 rugby ball per team.

HOW TO PLAY

- Players line up in their teams behind the start line.

- The player at the head of the line is the ball carrier.

- The ball carrier runs to the 10m line and back, performing skills (see below) along the way.

- The ball is handed over to the next player in line who performs a different set of skills and so on.

Skills to perform

1. Run to the line and score a try then run back and pass to next player.

2. Pass the ball around the body twice while running to the 10m and start lines.

3. Throw the ball in the air and clap before catching it at the 10m and start lines. Then pass to next in line.

4. Ground the ball with both hands halfway across, run to the 10m line, turn and pick up the ball with both hands on the way back.

5. Run to the 10m line, stop, raise one knee and pass the ball under that knee without dropping it. Repeat at the halfway point on the way back.

6. There are many possibilities with this exercise depending on the capabilities of the players.

DISABLED CHILDREN

If a child has very reduced mobility or is in a wheelchair give her/him a list of the exercises, assign a team, and then she/he can give the call for each player's drill as a reminder before the start. Remember to start at Exercise 3 on the team's second drill (see coaching tips below). This will allow the coach or teacher to concentrate on skills development.

COACHING TIPS

- Make sure that the players know which exercise they will be performing before the start. Demonstrate if necessary.

- Keep teams small to maximise the activity.

- When all five players have completed their ball handling exercise and there is time to repeat, start at Exercise 3 so the players all have a different task to do.

- Perform the skills correctly; no cutting corners or the player has to go back and start again.

VARIATIONS

Easy

Choose one skill that all the players in the team perform.

Advanced

Apply a more difficult range of skills and set a time limit for each team to perform these skills.

6. Tag attack! (all players)

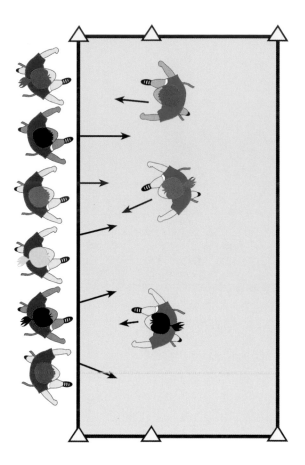

AIMS

● To improve evasion and tagging skills, and to find space.

PLAYERS/EQUIPMENT

● Whole pitch – 60m × 30m.

● Markers for a 20m position on the 30m line.

● Players divided into attackers and taggers.

- One tagger to two attackers.

- All players wearing belts/tags.

HOW TO PLAY

- The attackers line up across the length of the pitch on the sideline with a 2m gap between each.

- The taggers line up across the width of the field of play 20m from their defence line – one tagger to every two attackers.

- If necessary a second attacker team can be formed.

- On the coach/teacher's call 'Go!' the attackers run towards the attacker's defence line which is the opposite 60m line.

- The taggers must try to tag as many of the attackers as they can.

- The attackers must run into space to avoid being tagged.

- When all attackers have reached the defence line their tags are returned and the taggers resume their position on the 20m line.

- If there is another attacking team the players who have already run stay behind the defence line out of the way while this team runs.

- When all the attacking teams have had a run they can start again.

- After several turns the taggers can be swapped.

DISABLED CHILDREN

If a child has very reduced mobility or is in a wheelchair then he/she can give the call for each team to start. He/she can also keep a record of how many tags are taken on each run, which will show whether teams are improving with each run. This will allow the coach to concentrate on skills development.

COACHING TIPS

Encourage the attackers to:

- Find space and avoid running into other players.

- Switch places on subsequent turns so that the same taggers aren't targeting the same players each time.

- Keep a tally of how many times players are tagged.

Encourage the taggers to:

- Select a target, keep their heads up, and focus on the tag.

- Avoid running into other players.

- Select a different player as a target each time.

VARIATIONS

Easy

Have more taggers.

Advanced

Players drop out after being tagged twice. Tags are not returned until the end of the session.

Exercises 7–9

The following are more advanced exercises for the more experienced players who have had several months to develop their skills.

7. Fast catch (all players)

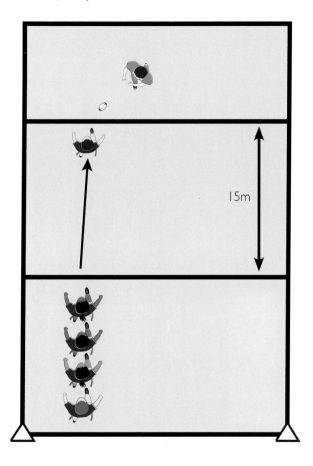

15m

AIMS

- To give players an opportunity to increase ability in catching the ball at speed – and improve both running and catching skills.

PLAYERS/EQUIPMENT

- A run of at least 15m in length for each team of players.

- Markers to divide runs if needed.

- Coach/teacher or other player at one end with six rugby balls.

- Players divided into attackers and taggers.

- One tagger to two attackers.

- All players wearing belts/tags.

HOW TO PLAY

- Passer – the coach or other player – is positioned on one knee at one end of run with six rugby balls.

- Players line up at the start of the run.

- Passer calls 'Go!' and the first attacker runs as fast as possible down the run towards the passer.

- As each player comes into the 'pass zone' at the end of the run the coach/other player passes the ball to them.

- Players must catch the ball at speed, run to a specified point and turn round to go back.

- When he/she reaches the passer again, each player then places the ball behind the passer.

- Good catching-at-speed skill is normally fairly quickly developed with this exercise.

DISABLED CHILDREN

As this is a fast game, some disabled children may not be able to keep up with the runners so they can be the passers. Or allowances can be made by coaches/teachers for a slower game.

COACHING TIPS

- This is an exercise to quicken players' running and catching responses, so it is important that players run at full speed down the line towards the passer.

- Players should be discouraged from slowing down or stopping when they come to catch the ball.

- Slow players can be accompanied on their run-up by a coach to encourage faster running.

8. Pass on the line (played in pairs)

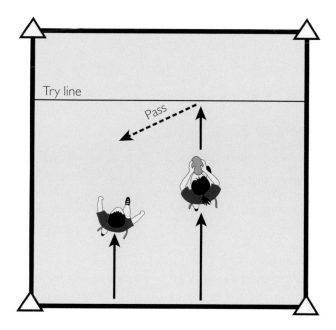

AIMS

- To encourage players to pass the ball near to the try line – when they are normally least likely to do so!

PLAYERS/EQUIPMENT

- A run at least 20m long.

- Try line for touch down.

- Players in pairs – a ball carrier and catcher.

- One size 3 rugby ball per pair.

HOW TO PLAY

- Players line up at the start of the run in pairs.

- One is the ball carrier, positioned just in front of their partner, who is the catcher.

- On a signal from the coach, the paired players run fast from a standing start towards the try line.

- As the front runner and ball carrier nears the try line, she/he turns and quickly passes the ball to the follower.

- The follower catches the ball and touches down over the line.

- Pairs of players do this in turn.

COACHING TIPS

- This exercise encourages the ball carrier to be aware of the follower and the follower to be aware of their partner in front.

- Players should be encouraged to turn quickly and pass accurately. This requires the follower to keep up with the ball carrier and to be ready to catch the ball and touch down over the line.

- In the early stages of this exercise, the coach will find it necessary to maintain proper distance between the carrier and follower, but with practice, the follower will learn to judge this distance for themselves, even calling for the ball as they come up near to the try line.

9. Pick and go

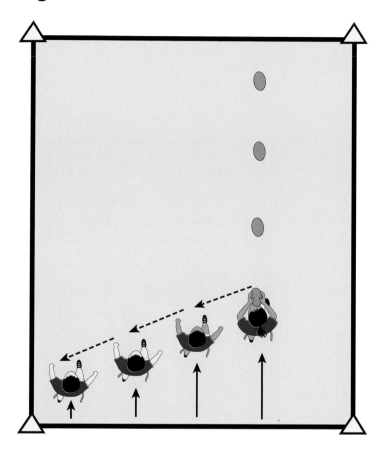

AIMS

- To practise picking up and passing at speed and to develop touch-down skills for scoring a try.

PLAYERS/EQUIPMENT

- The whole pitch.

- Try line for touch down.

- Players in teams of three or four.

- One size 3 rugby ball per team.

HOW TO PLAY

- Three or four rugby balls are placed in a line running up towards the goal line with a suitable running space between them.

- Players line up on the opposite side of the pitch in teams.

- On the coach/teacher's call of 'Go!' the first player runs at full speed from a standing start towards the first ball in line, followed by the other team players.

- The first player picks up the first rugby ball and passes it to the player behind.

- This player then passes it to the player behind her/him and so on to the last player in the team, who retains the ball.

- The first player runs on to pick up the second ball, and this passing back is repeated but this time the last-but-one player holds on to the ball as the last player in the team already has a ball.

- When all the other players in the team have a ball the first player picks up the final ball and, holding it in both hands, runs to the try line and touches down.

- The others in the team do this in turn until all players have grounded their ball.

DISABLED CHILDREN

As this is a fast game, some lesser abled children may not be able to keep up with the runners so allowances can be made by coaches/teachers for a slower game. For children in wheelchairs, they can referee near the try line by ensuring that the teams pick up pass and touch down correctly, and they can judge which team is the fastest.

COACHING TIPS

- This is an exercise for teams and requires cooperation, so ensure that the players know this but don't allow any criticism from players about other players.

- Run with struggling teams and help them out if necessary.

VARIATIONS

Easy

Have small teams and help out where required.

Advanced

Encourage really fast running and handling and swap players round to different teams, which requires them to react to different players.

6 FUN AND GAMES

These games are suitable for both clubs and schools, but for schools they are related to the National Curriculum Key Stages 1 and 2, and can be used as part of lesson plans. For full lesson plans and more information about the NC KS 2 see Chapter 7 (pages 115–135).

General points

Tag rugby is played by very young children and the most important factor of the game is that they enjoy it while improving their fitness and developing all the necessary skills for team and competition levels, and fulfilling the National Curriculum requirements. Drills and exercises can become very repetitive and lack the stimulus of variety and the action of games, where something different is happening all the time.

Drills also lack group interaction which helps to develop a sense of team spirit. Exercises and drills do have a place in tag rugby; indeed, they are vital in improving fitness so that when a game is played the players do not tire before the end of the session or match. However, too much exercise of a particular kind can strain young muscles and put the players off. If it's seen as a drudge they won't want to participate or they'll play reluctantly or badly. Fire them up and they'll be bursting with enthusiasm.

ORGANISATION

Before you begin a lesson or coaching session be absolutely sure how it is going to be organised and what you are going to do in the time allotted. This involves tailoring your activities to the playing area, the number of children in your class or club, and the amount of time you have. Use the lesson plans in Chapter 7 and mix and match the activities as it suits you and as time allows.

NOT JUST FOR SCHOOLS

The lesson plans in Chapter 7 are not just for teachers. Coaches and clubs can use the photocopiable pages for their sessions too.

CHANGING INTO SPORTS KIT

Very young children can take a long time changing into their sports kits, and you may find that most of the lesson goes while they struggle to put their kit on. It may be worth your while spending some time at the very beginning of your first lessons to concentrate on getting them to change quickly. In particular, doing up sports shoelaces can be a nightmare. Either get them to wear Velcro straps or encourage them to learn how to tie laces for themselves as quickly as possible.

CHECKS

Ensure that the pitch is laid out and that you have all items of equipment needed.

When children are running around enjoying themselves they don't always see problems but if you organise them properly, they will know that uncontrolled boisterous behaviour can lead to injury, and then they will play safely.

They must learn to respond to your commands immediately. This a not only a matter of establishing your authority; it is also for their safety. When you blow your whistle and ask players to stop, insist that all the players cease activity, stand still, and are listening to you.

Remind them of the rules, which do not allow barging or any other physical contact. Tagging involves only taking the tag. Neither the tagger nor the tagged player may fend off, or pull at clothing to avoid or take a tag.

A reward system is helpful, with stars or similar being awarded for effort and achievement. If you're running a club then perhaps you can award a small prize to the player who has achieved the most at the end of the season. This does not have to be the best player. It can be the player who has made the best effort and best progress.

All the games mentioned in the lesson plans are detailed below.

1. Spider's Web (all players or teams)

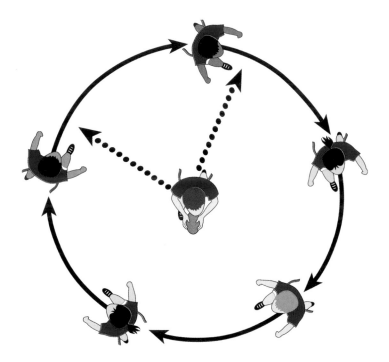

AIM

● To improve ball passing and handling skills.

PLAYERS/EQUIPMENT

● One size 3 rugby ball per team.

● Teams of 5 or 6 are fine but this will depend on the space available so you can have as many players per team as your space allows but more players may need a bigger circle and will be further away from Spider. Spider is in the centre, and the other players form a circle or web 2m or more from Spider. Make sure there is a good space between each player making up the web.

HOW TO PLAY

Spider stands still, holding the ball in both hands, and the other players form a circle around Spider, well spaced out from one another. Spider shouts 'Go!' and they start to run clockwise in a circle at a slow jogging pace. After a few seconds Spider shouts 'Stop!' and they stop running. Spider then passes the ball to a player who is either opposite or behind, but not in front, of him or her. That player catches the ball with both hands, passes back to Spider who shouts 'Go!' again. Spider must pass to a different player for each pass.

When Spider passes to the last player to catch a pass in any game that player becomes the new Spider and the game restarts.

COACHING TIPS

Encourage players to:

- Keep a good space between each other.

- Pass behind or across rather than forward but don't penalise absolute beginners who make forward passes.

- Stop if the ball goes to ground. All the players should wait until the ball catcher has retrieved the ball before starting to run again.

- Not to make any jeering comments about a player who drops a ball or halts the flow of play.

- Act in a sporting manner and adopt a team spirit.

DISABLED CHILDREN

If you have a child who uses a wheelchair or has reduced mobility this is an ideal game for his/her participation because the child can sit in a wheelchair, or on a chair, and be the Spider. The ball can be passed and caught from this position. Once there is a change of Spider, and if the surface is suitable and there is a gentle walking pace, then it may be possible for this child to join in with other players to form the web.

VARIATIONS

Easy

● Spider circles round on the spot while the players stand still.

● Spider shouts 'Pass!' when ready to pass and must pass to a different player each time.

● Or as above, but the player who has caught the ball turns and passes it to the player behind him/her until all the players forming the circle have had a chance to catch the ball. Then it is passed back to Spider, who starts again.

Advanced

● The players do not stop running when the ball is passed.

● The ball catcher passes back to Spider.

● Spider immediately passes the ball to the next player who passes back to Spider and so on.

● When all the players have caught the ball the last one becomes the new Spider.

● With each new Spider, the players run in the opposite direction from before.

SAFETY CONSIDERATIONS

Each set of players must have sufficient room to move around. If space is limited then increase the number of players in each set. Alternatively, have only one Spider in the middle and all the players around in a circle. When a player has caught and passed the ball back to Spider, she/he drops out of that session and sits or stands quietly to one side.

If a ball is dropped, Spider shouts 'Stop!' and all players immediately stop running until it is retrieved and held correctly in both hands before the game is restarted.

If the playing surface is hard you may consider that a walking pace is more appropriate than running.

2. Scarecrow Tag (teams or all players together)

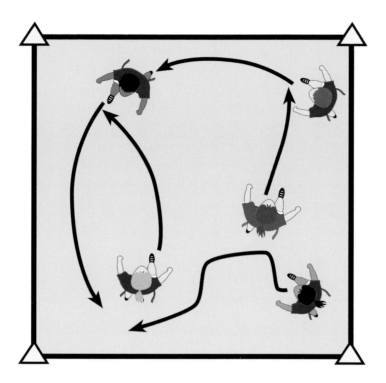

AIMS

- To develop running, tagging, and evasion skills.

PLAYERS/EQUIPMENT

- Grids of 5m × 5m laid out with markers or cones.

- Groups of five.

- Tags for all players.

HOW TO PLAY

One player is the defender, the other four are attackers. Attackers must find themselves space and run in any direction trying to avoid being tagged. The defender takes as many tags as possible. When a tag is taken he/she calls 'Tag!' and must then hand back the tag. On the tag call, the tagged player must stand still, reaffix the tag and then stand still with arms outstretched. To release their team-mate, another attacker must crawl under an arm of the tagged player.

DISABLED CHILDREN

Scarecrow tag may not be suitable for some children with reduced mobility. In this case, ask them to be the collector for the tags. The tagger must hand the tag to the collector who will then hand it back to the tagged player. (In the advanced version two tags from the same player are collected before being handed back.) The collector may also be able to keep the score of tags taken from individual players so that the players know how many times they've been tagged.

COACHING TIPS

- Attackers must keep their heads up and look for space.

- The defender should focus on the attacker's tag.

- Ensure that tags are handed back and not thrown down.

VARIATIONS

Easy
Use a smaller grid, and to free a tagged player an attacker must run under the outstretched arms of the tagged player and shout 'Free!'

Advanced
The defender must remove both tags from the same attacker before moving on to a different player.

3. Weavers (teams of 5 or 6)

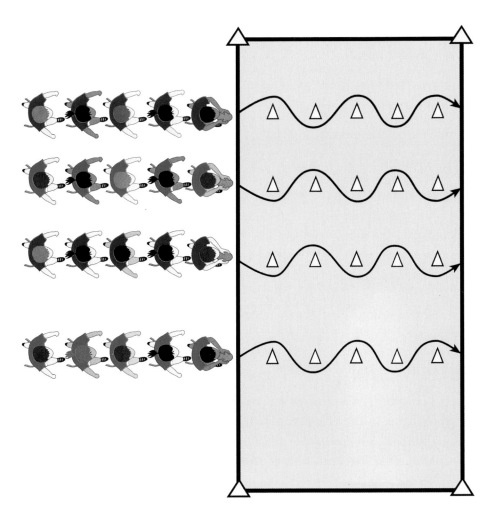

AIMS

- To learn how to weave/sidestep and avoid being tagged.

- To score a try.

PLAYERS/EQUIPMENT

- Markers such as cones or discs placed in a straight line across the pitch at regular intervals for each team.

- Put the markers across either the width of the pitch between the two sidelines (shorter distance) or the length of the pitch between the two try lines (longer) depending on the age and ability of the players.

- One size 3 ball per team.

- Divide into teams of equal numbers lined up behind the leader at the edge of the pitch, 5 or 6 to each team.

- Leader has the ball in both hands.

HOW TO PLAY

When signalled to start, the first player in line starts to weave in and out of the cones with the ball in both hands. When she/he reaches the opposite line the ball is grounded. The ball is then picked up by the same player and held in both hands as the player weaves back to her/his team and then passes to the next player in line. The ball passer then goes to the back of the line. The action is repeated until all players in the team have had their turn.

Allow one point for a successful try (where there are no infringements).

DISABLED CHILDREN

Weavers is probably not suitable for children with reduced mobility but you can assign them either to a particular team, or the teams in general, to watch out for infringements and alert the teams if an infringement has taken place. Let the players know that this is not being criticising of their play but being helpful in order for them to improve their play.

COACHING TIPS

Make sure that the players:

- Hold and pass the ball correctly, using both hands.

- Ground the ball correctly beyond the line, staying on their feet, bending over and not diving.

- Weave in and out of the markers without missing any out, touching or running over them.

- Start again if there are any infringements

VARIATIONS

Easy

Have fewer markers and/or have the markers more widely spaced.

Advanced

Have the cones closer together and set a time limit for the teams to finish within, and a point for any infringement. This score is deducted from the team's try score. When the teams play this game again they can aim for fewer dropped balls and more points.

4. Pass the Parcel (teams of 5)

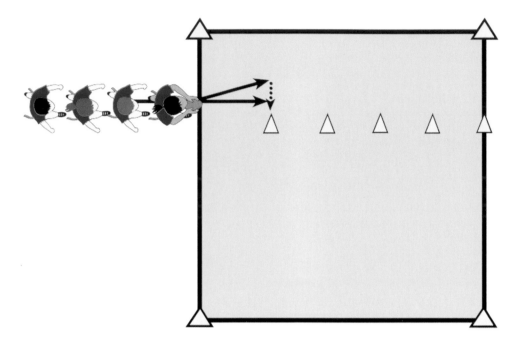

AIMS

- To improve passing and support play.

- Learning to take the ball on the run.

- To run 25m carrying and passing the ball as a team.

PLAYERS/EQUIPMENT

- Teams of 5.

- Markers showing 25m line on width of the pitch.

- Markers for each corner of the pitch.

- Markers for each team spaced at 5m intervals across the pitch.

- One size 3 ball per team.

HOW TO PLAY

Teams line up at the edge of the pitch. The player at the head of the team carries the ball first; he or she runs to the 5m marker, stops, and holds out the ball for the next player to take. When the ball is held out, the next player in line runs to the ball carrier, takes the ball and runs on to the next 5m marker and holds out the ball. The player holding out the ball stays in position by his/her marker. The next player in line should begin running when the player in front reaches the first 5m marker. The last player in the team should take the ball and score a try after reaching the 25m line.

When the game is finished, four players should be standing still by their markers and the fifth should have scored a try. Repeat with the try scorer heading the team each time to give each player a chance to score a try.

DISABLED CHILDREN

A disabled child who cannot participate in Pass the Parcel could be assigned to a team either to ensure that the ball is grounded correctly, or to call 'Go!' when a player has reached the 5m marker and it's time for the next player to begin the run. In the advanced version, this child could record the try score for a particular team.

COACHING TIPS

- Players must keep a 5m distance between each other.

- Remind the ball carriers to stop at the next 5m marker and hold out the ball.

- Encourage the players to take the ball without slowing down or stopping.

- The last player always scores a try to finish the game.

- Award a point to the team which finishes first in each game.

- Congratulate all teams on their effort and encourage improvement for the games to follow.

VARIATIONS

Easy

Walking or gentle jogging pace.

Advanced

Instead of standing still at the marker, the player who has passed the ball runs to the back of the line and play is continuous for a set period of time. Make a note of the team which has kept to the rules and scored the most tries.

5. Bulldog Baggers (all players)

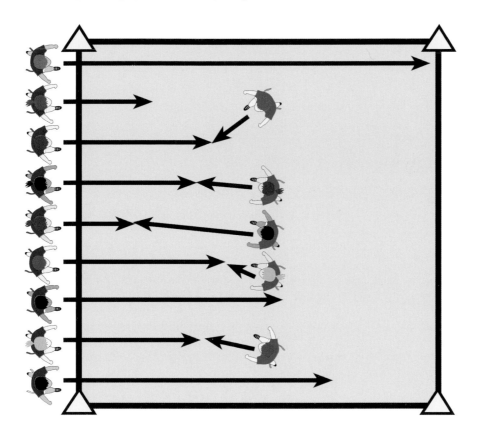

AIMS

- To improve running and evasion skills.

- To improve defending and tagging skills.

PLAYERS/EQUIPMENT

- Large grid of 30m × 30m, marked in the corners.

- Group of 5 defenders.

- All other players in one large group.

- Tag belts/tags.

HOW TO PLAY

The 5 defenders, known as bulldogs, are at the halfway point and fan out across the pitch. The rest of the players are the attackers and, on the coach's call, they try to run past the bulldogs to the opposite side of the pitch without being tagged. The bulldog defenders try to tag the attackers as they pass. Once tagged, a player joins the defenders as a bulldog. When all the attackers who haven't been tagged have lined up again, and all the tagged players have taken up their positions at the halfway point, the coach starts the game again.

DISABLED CHILDREN

A disabled child who cannot participate in Bulldog Baggers could be assigned to ensuring that the players keep to the rules and do not fend off others, grab clothing, or infringe in any other way. Or see the Easy option below.

COACHING TIPS

- Encourage the attackers to look for space to run to avoid being tagged.
- Encourage the bulldogs to select an attacker for tagging rather than rushing about aimlessly, and to keep their heads up.
- All tags must be handed back after a successful tagging.
- Bulldogs should try to defend in one line as a team.

VARIATIONS

Easy

Attackers have to hop on one leg. This could enable those with limited mobility to take part.

Advanced

- The same 5 players remain as Bulldogs and are not joined by tagged players. Once tagged a player has to drop out of the game until the next game starts.
- Bulldogs have to tag the same player twice before they drop out of the game.

6. Run Rabbit Run (teams of 6 v 4)

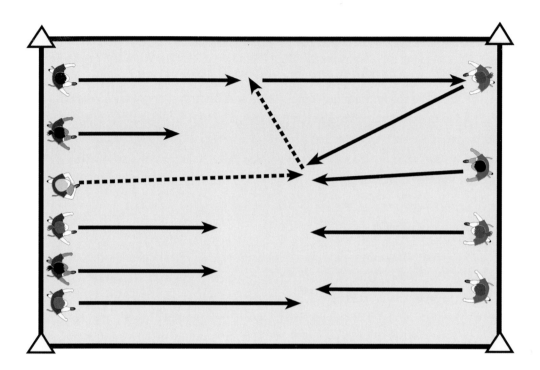

AIMS

- For attackers to run into space, to avoid being tagged and to score a try for their team.

- To make the right decisions on where to run and who to pass to once tagged.

- To keep play flowing.

- Defenders can improve their tagging and defending skills.

PLAYERS/EQUIPMENT

- Pitch of 30m × 20m with markers at the four corners, a centre line, and a 7m line either side of centre line.

- Teams of 6 attackers against 4 defenders.

- Tag belts/tags.

- One size 3 ball per team.

HOW TO PLAY

The four defenders fan out across the width of the pitch at least 7m from the centre line, in the half of the pitch that they are defending. The six attackers fan out as a team, with the ball carrier on the centre line and the other players behind. Start the game with a free pass at the centre. The attacking team must try to run past the defenders to score a try. If tagged, the player must pass the ball backwards to a team-mate within three strides or three seconds. After a tag the defender must hand the tag back and retreat to stay onside, and must not attempt to intercept of obstruct a pass.

DISABLED CHILDREN

A disabled child who cannot participate in Run Rabbit Run could be assigned to make the call for the first team, then the other teams in order, to line up in their positions ready for the game to start. When all players are in position she/he can then start the game by calling 'Go!' She/he can also keep track of the number of tags taken and tries scored for each team. This will free up the teacher or coach to concentrate on ensuring that infringements do not occur. If they do, the teacher or coach should draw attention to the infringement so that players learn the correct way to play tag rugby.

COACHING TIPS

- Attackers must try to dodge the defenders.

- Pass if tagged, if about to be tagged, or if a team-mate is in a better position.

- The ball carrier's team must stay behind the ball.

- The team should communicate with each other.

- Defenders should keep their heads up to concentrate on whom to tag.

- They should always hand the tag back after a successful tag.

- It may be helpful for the taggers to keep a tally of how many tags made for each team.

VARIATIONS

Easy

Have 7 attackers to 4 defenders per team.

Advanced

Have teams of 5 against 5, or 4 against 4.

7

LESSON PLANS

The following timed lesson plans can be used very effectively by both coaches and teachers, either for 30 or 60 minutes, or you can extract whichever exercises suit. However, remember to keep to the principles of warming up and warming down at the beginning and end of each lesson, coaching session or game. If you are not a teacher go directly to Lesson 1 on page 118, missing out the National Curriculum notes.

The National Curriculum Key Stage 1 and 2 for PE for England

The National Curriculum stresses the importance of physical education for pupils of all ages in schools. PE can involve a range of activities, including sports and tag rugby meets the KS 1 and 2 requirements.

It is important to note that getting involved in lifelong physical activity is encouraged from the outset and tag rugby can be played very comfortably by 5 year olds.

The following by no means contains the complete requirements and details of the National Curriculum, but it will give you an idea of what is expected of you as regards tag rugby. For full details go to the government's website:

www.education.gov.uk/schools/teachingandlearning/curriculum/primary

KEY STAGE 1

During Key Stage 1 pupils build on their natural enthusiasm for movement, using it to explore and learn about their world. They start to work and play with other pupils in pairs and small groups. By watching, listening and experimenting, they develop their skills in movement and coordination, and enjoy expressing and testing themselves in a variety of situations.

Knowledge, skills and understanding

Children need to acquire knowledge, skills and understanding and teachers need to ensure that when evaluating and improving performance, they make connections between developing, selecting and applying skills, tactics and compositional ideas, and fitness and health.

Amongst the many and varied skills to be acquired and developed by pupils in KS1, tag rugby can contribute by teaching pupils to:

- Remember and repeat simple skills and actions.

- Use these skills and actions in sequence and combination.

- Vary the way they perform skills by using simple tactics and movement phrases.

- Describe what they have done.

- Observe, describe and copy what others have done.

- Appreciate how important it is to be active.

- Travel with, send and receive a ball in different ways.

- Use simple tactics for attacking and defending.

This fits in very well with tag rugby because beginners will be learning, developing and improving a whole range of skills including running, ball control, hand-eye coordination, passing the ball, evasion tactics, working in pairs and being part of a team.

KEY STAGE 2

When children have progressed to this this stage it's obvious that they enjoy being active, and using their creativity and imagination in organised physical activity is great fun. They learn new skills, find out how to use them in different ways, and link them to make actions, phrases and sequences of movement. They enjoy communicating, collaborating and competing with each other. They develop an understanding of how to succeed in different activities, and learn how to evaluate and recognise their own success.'

Knowledge, skills and understanding

This is the same as for KS 1 but tag rugby can further contribute to KS 2 by teaching pupils to:

- Consolidate their existing skills and use new ones.

- Perform actions and skills with more consistent control and quality.

- Plan, use and adapt strategies and tactics for individual, pair, small-group and small-team activities.

- Identify what makes a performance effective.

- Suggest improvements based on this information.

- Have a knowledge and understanding of fitness and health.

- Realise how exercise affects the body in the short term.

- Warm up and prepare appropriately for different activities.

- Understand why physical activity is good for their health and well-being.

- Understand why wearing appropriate clothing and being hygienic is good for health and safety.

- Use skills and tactics suitable for attacking and defending.

- Work with others to organise and keep games going.

VERY YOUNG SCHOOL CHILDREN?

If your class has very young children under 7 and there are more than 20 of them then you will probably spend most of your time getting them changed! You may literally have only 5 or 10 minutes of the lesson left. If this happens you will have to select one activity from the lesson plans. I would suggest that you explain the game first, then concentrate on how to hold the ball correctly, pass it while standing still in pairs, pass it when running in pairs, and how to tag. Once these skills have been practised you can use them in fun team games and then they'll be ready for a game itself.

Lesson 1: absolute beginners – 30 or 60 mins

Lesson 1 for absolute beginners follows in a photocopiable lesson plan which you can use. You will also be advised where to find more detailed information for the exercises, drills and games in these plans.

Note: for the 30 minute Lessons 1–3 you will need to use 1a and 2a in order to catch up with the skills covered in the 60 minute lessons. After this it is assumed that your players will know how to score a try, how to tag and how to pass and you can follow through from Lesson 4 onwards.

TAG RUGBY: WHAT IS IT?

It is essential that the children know what tag rugby is and how they should play the game so it will pay off if you spend time initially explaining the basic principles, using the rules laid out in Chapter 2. It will also be very helpful to use some of the pupils to demonstrate what you are saying.

THE OBJECT OF THE GAME IS TO SCORE A TRY

Both hands on the ball, over the try line, no diving.

HOW TO TAG

It is essential that the players know how a tag belt is worn correctly and how to take a tag.

NO TACKLING, KICKING OR CONTACT OF ANY KIND

Explain that tag rugby for minis is not like junior or senior rugby to ensure younger children do not get injured, but make sure they know how exciting this game can be.

FREE PASSES

Explain why and how free passes are taken.

WARMING UP AT THE START

Begin gently or there is the risk of muscle strain or other injury. The whole object of warming up is to prepare the body for sustained energetic exercise. So the players need to work up to this in a controlled way. Mix exercises at a gentle jogging pace with those that can be done standing still, depending on the age and skills of the children.

WARMING DOWN AT THE END

Always end with a few minutes of warm down if possible.
Note: All lessons allow time for changing.

Lesson 1: For absolute beginners

Duration: 30 or 60 minutes

Objective: Players will learn how the game is played (30 mins) and how to pass the ball (60 mins).

Activity	Equipment	Action	Notes
1. What is tag rugby? Explaining the game (15 mins)	Size 3 rugby balls, tag belts and tags.	Full class seated and concentrating, volunteers in pairs.	Demonstrate the rules as in Chapter 2 using volunteers. Test them if time.
2. Warm down (30 min lesson) or warm up (60 min lesson) (5/10 mins)		Touch toes 5 or 10 times. Sidestep × 10 with right leg leading, then 10 with left.	Begin gently, no muscle strain. Repeat these two exercises if time.
END OF 30-MIN LESSON. FOR NEXT LESSON GO TO 1A.			
3. How to hold and pass the ball (5 mins)	Size 3 rugby balls, tags/belts.	In pairs, standing still, the player holds ball in both hands and passes to partner opposite.	Throw the ball gently with both hands. Catch with both hands.
4. Game: Spider's Web (ball-passing skills) (10/15 mins)	Size 3 rugby ball per team.	All players, or teams of 5 or 6. Spider in middle with ball, players form circle, jog, Spider shouts 'Stop!' and passes ball, ball passed back. Repeat.	See page 98 for more information on Spider's Web. Stand still to pass, or vary pace, or vary game; for example, Spider can shout 'Pass' and the players can catch ball and pass straight back to Spider without stopping.

5. Warm down (5 mins max)		• Touch toes: legs straight, bend over, touch toes. • Relax: lie down, relax all muscles and think of the best thing that's happened this week.	Remind them that warm down is important. A very quiet moment at end of a lesson is good for self-discipline.

END OF 60-MINUTE LESSON. FOR NEXT LESSON GO TO 2.

Lesson 1A: Getting started

Duration: 30 minutes

Objective: Players will learn how to hold and pass the ball.

> **Tip:**
> Not much time? Cut exercise time and concentrate on developing ball-handling skills, standing still and running.

Activity	Equipment	Action	Notes
1. Warm up (5 mins max)		• Swing round: stand still with arms outstretched and swing arms round from side to side. • Gentle jog round field of play, large or small.	Make space. Keep legs still and move upper body gently – don't twist your back.
2. How to hold and pass the ball (5 mins)	Size 3 rugby balls, tags/belts.	In pairs, standing still, players hold ball in both hands and pass to partner opposite.	Throw ball gently, catch with both hands.
3. Game: Spider's Web (ball-passing skills) (10/ 15 mins)	Size 3 rugby ball per team.	All players or teams of 5 or 6. Spider in middle with ball, players form circle, jog, Spider shouts 'Stop!' and passes ball, ball passed back. Repeat.	See page 98 for more information on Spider's Web. Stand still to pass, or vary pace, or vary game; for example, Spider can shout 'Pass' and the players can catch ball and pass straight back to Spider without stopping.

4. Warm Down (5 mins)		Pedal Power: Lie on back and pedal legs in the air. Relax: lie down, relax all muscles and think of the best thing you've read this week.	Try to make a big arc with your feet. A very quiet moment at end of lesson is good for self-discipline.

END OF 30-MINUTE LESSON 1A. NEXT LESSON 2: HOW TO TAG.

Lesson 2: How to tag

Duration: 30 or 60 minutes

Objective: Players will learn how to tag and practice ball carrying (30min and 60min).

Tip:

Not much time? Cut exercise time and concentrate on How to Tag.

Activity	Equipment	Action	Notes
1. **Warm up: Figure of Eight (ball-carrying practice)** (5/10 mins)	Size 3 rugby balls, tags/belts.	Three players in a line. Ball carrier 1 jogs/walks gently in figure of eight round others, passes ball to 2. Repeat with players 2 and 3.	Avoid touching other players. Carry ball with both hands. Repeat until time's up.
2. **Weavers (avoid being tagged** (5/10 mins)	Markers in straight line across pitch at regular intervals.	Teams of 5 or 6. Ball carrier weaves in and out of cones, scores try, weaves back through and passes to next in line, who repeats drill.	Two hands on ball, ground correctly. No touching markers. Start again if infringement.
3. **Tagging. (learn how to tag)** (10 mins)	Tags/tag belts.	In pairs, step forward taking tag, hold up, shout 'Tag!' Continue until both tags of each pair have been taken and reaffixed. Practise running and taking tag.	Tag belts to be worn correctly. Pairs stand few paces opposite partner. Only the defenders to take tags.
4. **Warm down (If you are using the 60-minute lesson plan, miss this stage out and go to step 4)** (5 mins max)		• Touch toes 5 or 10 times. • Relax: lie down, relax all muscles and think of the best thing you've read this week.	• Begin gently, no muscle strain. • A very quiet moment at end of lesson is good for self-discipline.

END OF 30-MIN LESSON. FOR NEXT LESSON GO TO 2A.

5. Game: Scarecrow Tag (running, tagging and evasion skills) (15 mins)	Grids of 5m × 5m, tag belts, tags.	Teams of 5, or all players. One player is defender/tagger; the others run to avoid tag. When the tagger takes a tag, he/she calls 'Tag!' then hands tag back. Tagged player stands still, arms outstretched until another player crawls under an outstretched arm.	See page 101 for more information on Scarecrow Tag. Defender should focus on the attacker's tag. Attackers must keep heads up and look for space. Tags must be handed back/not thrown down.
6. Warm down (5/10 mins)		• Gentle jog round field of play, large or small area. • Swing round: stand still with arms outstretched and swing arms round from side to side.	Keep legs still and move upper body gently – don't twist your back.

END OF 60-MINUTE LESSON. FOR NEXT LESSON GO TO 3.

Lesson 2A: How to tag

Duration: 30 miuntes

Objective: Players will practise and improve tagging skills.

Activity	Equipment	Action	Notes
1. Warm up (5/10 mins)		Gentle walk or jog.	Tailor the pace and area to the age and fitness of the players.
2. Game: Scarecrow Tag (running, tagging and evasion skills) (15 mins)	Grids of 5m × 5m, tag belts, tags.	Teams of 5, or all players. One player is defender/tagger; the others run to avoid tag. When the tagger takes a tag, he/she calls 'Tag!' then hands tag back. Tagged player stands still, arms outstretched until another player crawls under an outstretched arm.	See page 101 for more information on Scarecrow Tag. Defender should focus on the attacker's tag. Attackers must keep heads up and look for space. Tags must be handed back/not thrown down.
3. Warm down (5 mins)		Swing round: stand still with arms outstretched and swing arms round from side to side.	Keep legs still and move upper body gently – don't twist your back.

END OF LESSON 2A. FOR NEXT LESSON GO TO 3.

Lesson 3: How to score a try

Duration: 30 or 60 minutes

Objective: Players will learn how to score a try.

Activity	Equipment	Action	Notes
1. Warm up: Conga (skills for passing and support play) (5/10 mins)	Size 3 balls, grids of 20m × 20m.	Teams of 5 in a line, one ball per team. Ball carrier leads and can run in any direction; the other players follow. When coach calls 'Pass!', the ball carrier passes to the next player. Passer goes to the end of the line and the new ball carrier leads. Continue.	See page 77 for more information about Conga. Run into space, avoiding other teams. Follow ball carrier and leave a good space between players. Catch the ball without slowing down.
2. How to score a try (15 mins/20 mins)	Size 3 rugby balls, tags/belts.	Pairs of teams with up to 5 players per team line up on opposite sidelines. Ball carrier starts at the front of one line and runs to the player at the head of the opposite line, grounds the ball with both hands and goes to the back of the line. Next player picks up the ball and runs to ground it on the opposite team line. Continue.	Hold the ball firmly in both hands. Ground the ball with two hands, and with both feet on the pitch. Ensure that all players have the chance to ground the ball at least once.

3. Warm down **(If you are using the 60-minute lesson plan, miss out this stage and go to step 4.)** (5 mins)		• Pedal power: lie on back and pedal legs in the air. • Relax: lie down, relax all muscles and think of the best thing you've read this week.	• Try to make a big arc with your feet. • A very quiet moment at end of lesson is good for self-discipline.
END OF 30-MINUTE LESSON. FOR NEXT LESSON GO TO 4.			
4. Weavers (avoid being tagged) (5/10 mins)	Markers in straight line across pitch at regular intervals.	Teams of 5 or 6. Ball carrier weaves in and out of cones, scores try, weaves back through the markers and passes to next in line, who then performs the drill.	See page 103 for more information on Weavers. Two hands on ball, ground correctly. No touching markers. Start again if infringement.
5. Warm down (5 mins)		Swing round: stand still with arms outstretched and swing arms round from side to side.	Keep legs still and move upper body gently – don't twist your back.
END OF 60-MINUTE LESSON. FOR NEXT LESSON GO TO 4.			

Lesson 4: Let's play tag rugby!

Duration: 30 or 60 minutes

Objectives: Evasion practice and a game

Tip:
Lack of time? Warm up for 5 minutes, then go directly to step 3, missing out step 2

Activity	Equipment	Action	Notes
Warm up: Crossing the Channel (evasion, running and passing skills). (5/10 mins)	Channels of 20m × 15m and 20m × 5m, one size 3 rugby ball per team.	Teams of 4. First team run after ball carrier through narrow channel into wider channel, then fan out and pass the ball along the line. The next team follow when team ahead is in the wide channel.	See page 75 for more information on Crossing the Channel. Ball carrier should look ahead when running, but at the other player's position and hands when passing to them. Ball carrier should get ahead of their team in narrow channel for pass. All players should keep within easy passing range.
2. Let's play tag rugby!	Size 3 rugby balls, one per game, tag belts/tags. Bibs or different coloured tags for each team.	Play in teams of 4, 5, 6 or 7, with the same number of players in teams playing each other.	Remind children of basic rules of how to play. Switch players around if any team is 5 points or more ahead to even out play.

(15/25 mins: 5 or10 mins each half with a 2-minute interval)			If you have only one teacher or coach for more than 14 players, give two teams a 5-min game, while the others watch (if it's not too cold) or play one of the games in Chapter 6. Then swap your players round so that everyone gets a chance of a game with the coach.
5. Warm down (5/10 mins)		• Swing round: stand still with arms outstretched and swing arms round from side to side. • Pedal power: lie on back and pedal legs in the air.	Go gently after all that action.

END OF LESSON. FOR NEXT LESSON GO TO 5.

Lesson 5: Improving skills

Duration: 30 or 60 minutes

Objectives: To practice running and passing skills, working as a team and playing a game

---

Tip:

Lack of time? Warm up for 5 minutes, then choose either step 2 or step 3.

Activity	Equipment	Action	Notes
1. **Warm Up: Calling the Shots. (running/ passing skills, working as a team)** (5/10 mins)	Two adjacent channels of 20m × 10m, size 3 rugby balls.	Teams of 4. In the first channel, players fan out from ball carrier who calls 'Pass!' Fourth player bursts through for the pass; when in position, he or she calls 'Pass!' for the ball to be passed. Repeat in next channel.	See page 79 for more information on Calling the Shots. Make sure the players understand the game. Player should burst through to receive the pass at pace. Find space and don't bunch together. Listen to 'Pass!' calls.
2. **Game: Pass the Parcel (passing and support play)** (10 mins)	Straight line of 5m × 5m, size 3 rugby balls.	Teams of 5 in a line. Ball carrier runs to first marker and holds out the ball. The next player takes it, runs to the second marker and holds it out for the third player, and so on. The first player goes to the back of the line. The fifth player scores a try. Award a point to the team who finishes first.	See page 106 for more information on Pass the Parcel. Players must keep 5m between them. At each marker the ball is held out for next player. Congratulate all teams on their effort and improvement.

3. Let's play tag rugby!	Size 3 rugby balls, one per game, tag belts/tags. Bibs or different coloured tags for each team.	Play in teams of 4, 5, 6 or 7, with the same number of players in teams playing each other.	Remind children of basic rules of how to play. Switch players around if any team is 5 points or more ahead to even out play.
(15/25 mins: 5 or 10 mins each half with a 2-minute interval)			If you have only one teacher or coach for more than 14 players, give two teams a 5-min game, while the others watch (if it's not too cold) or play one of the games in Chapter 6. Then swap your players round so that everyone gets a chance of a game with the coach.

END OF 30-MINUTE LESSON. FOR NEXT LESSON GO TO 6.

5. Warm down		• Pedal power: lie on back and pedal legs in the air.	• Try to make a big arc with your feet.
(5/10 mins)		• Relax: lie down, relax all muscles and think of the best thing you've read this week.	• A very quiet moment at end of lesson is good for self-discipline.

END OF LESSON. FOR NEXT LESSON GO TO 6.

Lesson 6: Further skills

Duration: 30 or 60 minutes

Objectives: Running, evasion and tagging Skills and finding space

> **Tip:**
> Lack of time? Warm up for 5 minutes, then choose either step 2 or step 3.

Activity	Equipment	Action	Notes
1. **Warm up: Bulldog Baggers (defending, tagging, running and evasion)** (5/10 mins)	Tag belts/tags. Use the size of pitch you normally play on.	Team of 5 defenders, with the others in a large group. Bulldogs are defenders, the rest are attackers. Once tagged, a player becomes a Bulldog Bagger.	See page 109 for more information on Bulldog Baggers. Players should look for space to avoid being tagged. Bulldogs should select a target – no aimless running.
2. **It's a try! (multi-skills development)** (5/15 mins)	Markers marking out a line 10m from start line, size 3 rugby ball per team.	Teams of 5 line up behind try line. The ball carrier runs to the 10m line and back performing skills as directed by the coach, then passes to next player who repeats the drill, and so on.	See page 81 for ideas on exercises and drills. Demonstrate the exercises and make sure the players know which exercises they are doing.
3. **Tag Attack! (evasion and tagging skills, finding space)**	Markers marking out a 20m line on a 60m × 30m pitch, belts/tags.	One tagger to two attackers. Attackers run to 20m line and try to avoid being tagged. Another team of attackers can be waiting to start.	See page 84 for more information on Tag Attack!

(10/15 mins)			Taggers should keep their heads up, select their target and focus on the tag. Other players should look for space to avoid the tagger.
4. Warm down (5/10 mins)		• Pedal power: lie on back and pedal legs in the air. • Relax: lie down, relax all muscles and think of the best TV programme or film you've seen this week.	• Try to make a big arc with your feet. • A very quiet moment at end of lesson is good for self-discipline. No talking!

END OF LESSON.

8 REFEREEING

Where to start

So you've always wanted to be a referee, or maybe you have to be a referee because your school or club needs you: where do you start? Rugby's a complicated game, and if you haven't refereed a match before you may be worrying about the dizzying aspect of the rules in the professional game, but there's no need – tag rugby is really simple by comparison.

Naturally, before you can run out on to the field of play with whistle and notebook in hand, you are advised to undertake the Entry Level Referee Award (ELRA). The RFU strongly recommends that all referees, irrespective of the age group they are officiating, undertake the ELRA. However, if you are only interested in gaining an understanding of how to referee mini and midi rugby, then you could attend the RFU Mini Midi Refereeing course.

You can now book a refereeing course online.[1] Prior to attending the course, you will be required to complete the online iRB Rugby Ready programme.[2] You will then need

[1] www.rfu.com/coaches-and-referees
[2] www.irbrugbyready.com

to download your RugbyReady certificate and bring it with you to the course. You will not receive your Mini Midi course certificate until you have completed the RugbyReady programme, details of which can be found at:

www.rfu.co.uk/takingpart/referee/courses/accessinganelracourse

The ELRA is a three-stage award which will provide you with the key tools to referee competently.

If you choose to join a regional referee's society, then you will be required to complete all three stages of the ELRA. If you wish to remain within your own school, club or university, then you need only complete stages 1 and 2. These cover the following aspects of refereeing:

- Management and control.
- Problem solving.
- Refereeing the key phases of the game.
- Positioning and communication.
- Laws of the game.

Stages 1 and 2 focus on practical learning, giving you the opportunity to observe refereeing in practice and build confidence in your own skills on the field of play. A calendar is available with details of ELRA courses running near you.

WHAT NEXT?

If you wish to develop further as a referee once you have completed ELRA stages 1 and 2, your local referees' society is on hand to help.

Becoming a member of the many referees' societies means you will be appointed to a wide variety of games and have access to ongoing training, support and development opportunities. You will then be able to progress as far as your abilities and ambition allow. For information on joining, please contact your local society, and refer to the IRB (International Rugby Board) site, www.irb.com, for further material on refereeing.

The RFU Refereeing Pathway diagram is a useful document to show potential progress of referees through the ranks.

You will need to familiarise yourself with the rules (see Chapter 2, pages 23–37) and make sure you know them thoroughly. There's no time for hesitation in a running game: you have to make decisions quickly and correctly, which means you have to be absolutely sure of what you are doing as a referee. As time goes on, your experience will give you more confidence and enable you to relax and enjoy the games.

One point you can be sure of, which will help if you feel nervous, is that you will always know more than the players at this level. Show confidence and authority and explain your decision by referring to the rules, and everything should go well. Also, it stands to reason that the more games you referee the easier it will become.

YOU DON'T HAVE TO BE OLD TO BE A REFEREE

Young people from 14 years of age can become tag rugby referees. Find out how from this chapter and from the RFU's website.

YOU MEAN I CAN ENJOY BEING A REFEREE?

Absolutely! It all depends on you and your attitude. Admittedly, it's a big responsibility because the result, the flow of the game and the spirit in which it's played depend on your expertise, your interpretation of what's going on and your decisions. You may also be the subject of a little heckling from the sidelines or even some dissent from the players, but don't let any of that put you off. Being an efficient professional, and above all enjoying what you're doing, is really worthwhile because you are giving something to the young children of this country. All too often children get a terrible press and we only hear about their bad behaviour, but if the majority of children were uncontrollable, aggressive and worthless there would be complete chaos both in school and out of it. This does not happen. The majority of children are keen to learn and love participating in sports. If you love the game passionately it will inspire children.

Add to this the opportunity to travel to new venues, both locally and nationally, and to make new friends in the game and you'll understand how much you will get out of being a community referee.

IS IT DIFFICULT TO REFEREE?

Sometimes, especially when you first start out. However, there is a lot of help available from local referees' societies. If you have played the game you will already have knowledge of what is required, and one enormous advantage is that you will know what it's like to be a player, which means you'll be able to empathise with your young charges. As you become more experienced, the science and art of refereeing become easier. Nevertheless, every match presents you with a challenge, as no two matches are the same.

Support

Referees' societies have monthly meetings throughout the season where aspects of law and refereeing management are discussed. The RFU also has a development pathway for referees, touch judges, assessors and referee coaches. Each step along the pathway is supported by an award course.

So, your very first priorities are to:

- complete an accredited course for referees.

- learn the rules of the game thoroughly (see Chapter 2, pages 23–37).

Refereeing a game

EQUIPMENT NEEDED FOR REFEREEING TAG RUGBY

You won't need a suitcase for the equipment needed to referee a game of tag rugby, but there are, of course, some essentials:

- whistle – and you may need a second as a back-up.

- stopwatch – make sure you've practised with it before a match.

- notebook or paper for keeping the score.

- pen or pencil for recording the score and anything else of consequence that may happen during a game.

- different coloured sports shirt from either team playing.

- suitable sports shoes matched to the conditions of the playing surface. These will include trainers with good grip for hard surfaces, which may be dry impacted grassy areas as well as concrete or tarmac, and IRB-approved rugby boots for softer surfaces such as a playing field.

WHAT TO DO BEFORE PLAY BEGINS

Check:

- the playing area: is it safe and free from any debris or animal waste?

- the pitch: is it within dimensions laid out in the rules and are the lines clearly marked?

- the rugby ball: is it the right size? Do you need spares?

- the players: are there the same number of players in each team?

- watches and jewellery: ask the players to remove any items that could cause injury either to themselves or to other players

- shirts and tops: are they tucked securely into tracksuit bottoms or shorts?

- tags and belts: are the belt straps tucked in securely? Are the tags themselves hanging freely and not wrapped around the belt so they can be removed easily?

- mouthguards: these are always advisable, but the RFU insists on players having this protection in competitions. Encourage your players to be safe.

PROBLEMS?

Odd number of players

If you are a coach and also have to referee the game, and you find that you have an odd number of players, discuss this with the children and suggest that one of them helps you referee by becoming a touch judge for the first half of the game. This player could then swap with another player in the team for the second half. At least this way the extra player gets to play some of the time.

If there is no volunteer for this, ask the children to write their names on a piece of paper and fold it over. Put all these names into a container, give it a good stir and then draw out two pieces of paper. The first name out plays in the first half, the other is a touch judge and they change over for the second half.

Someone's not got the right kit

You will have to assess whether this child can play in what they have got. If you consider their clothing or footwear to be a safety issue you must not allow them to play, but if it's simply a matter of not having expensive trainers or not having the same kit as the others, there's no reason why the child cannot play.

Dissent and abuse of the referee

Dissent is when a player argues with the referee over a decision. This isn't likely to occur in a threatening or really serious manner by tag rugby players and abuse is more likely to come from the spectators, but it should always be nipped in the bud. Being a good sport is essential and arguing with decisions should not be tolerated at any level, even if that decision appears to be wrong. Encourage players to accept decisions gracefully and get on with the game. This can be reinforced when you are discussing the game of tag rugby with your players, or after a game, or on a bad weather day when you can't get a game going.

There are rare cases of abuse, but the RFU and Constituent Bodies penalise very heavily any player or club member shown to be abusive. All clubs have to agree to abide by the Code of Conduct for stopping the abuse of match officials (see the appendix).

Officials must always report in writing, to the club or CB (Constituent Body) welfare officer and/or society secretary, behaviour by adults that you feel contravenes RFU Child Protection Policy (see page 147 for more information on this). This may include the following:

- verbal bullying by coaches/parents/spectators.

- physical abuse by coaches/parents/spectators.

- inappropriate or aggressive contact by an adult to a young person.

- verbal abuse directed at the official by young people or adults.

Remember: the welfare of all young people is paramount.

STARTING THE GAME

If you have time before the match, gather the teams together and tell them how you expect them to behave:

- keeping to the rules.

- no bad language.

- no taunting or laughing at any other player.

- accepting the referee's decision without backchat.

- obeying the 7-metre rule.

- reversing decision for dissent.

- being a gracious winner and a good loser.

Also remind them about finding space and keeping to their positions.

DURING THE GAME

You should concentrate on:

- giving clear signals.

- scoring properly.

- forward passes.

- correct tagging.

- free pass rules.

- dead ball.

- knock-on.

- offside.

- dealing with injury.

- dealing with difficult players.

- time keeping.

Dealing with problems

Always blow your whistle to stop play and explain briefly and succinctly why you are doing this and what the infringement is. Watch out for the following:

- bad language – give a warning at first, then an on-pitch penalty (free pass) for the next offence.

- foul play – make it clear you will not accept this and why it is unacceptable, concentrating on safety and being a good sport, then award a free pass to the other side.

PUNISHING DISSENT IN THE SENIOR GAME

In senior rugby, if a player argues with a decision made by the referee, the referee may move the penalty spot 10 m forward as a further punishment for dissent. This can mean the difference between having to kick for a line out or being able to kick for a penalty goal, worth three points. It is very effective and virtually eliminates insults or arguments about the decision.

AT THE END OF THE GAME

Gather the players around, remind them of the score and congratulate the winners, but also praise both teams. Get the players to shake hands with the opposing team and then ask the winning team to form a tunnel so that they can applaud the losing team off the field; this will encourage good sporting behaviour.

9

SAFEGUARDING CHILDREN

Working with children is always very challenging and very rewarding, but if you are a coach, referee or anyone involved in tag rugby, whether on a professional or volunteer basis, then you are obliged by law to provide those children with the highest possible standard of care. This chapter contains essential information on the legal and moral requirements for anyone wishing to become involved with tag rugby, based on the RFU's own guidelines:

SAFEGUARDING CHILDREN

The safety of children and young adults is of paramount importance and the RFU takes the subject very seriously. We are committed to ensuring that young people, whatever their background, enjoy the game in a fun environment, safe from any kind of abuse. The Safeguarding Children page in the Managing Rugby section takes a broader look at what you can expect from the RFU. You can download a copy for your own use.

www.rfu.co.uk/managingrugby/safeguarding children

The RFU is very careful to ensure that these guidelines are understood and carried out. Although this may seem to be a common-sense matter, it isn't until you start looking at the issues that you realise there's much more to it than you think. The key principles on which this policy statement are based states:

- The welfare of the child or vulnerable adult is paramount.

- All participants regardless of age, gender, ability or disability, race, faith, size, language or sexual identity, have the right to protection from harm.

- All allegations and suspicions of harm will be taken seriously and responded to swiftly, fairly and appropriately.

- Everyone will work in partnership to promote the welfare, health and development of children and vulnerable adults.

- The interests of those who work or volunteer with children and vulnerable adults will be protected. However, the RFU knows that any procedure for children's welfare and protection is only as effective as the ability and skill of those who operate it. The RFU/ RFUW are therefore committed to effective recruitment and appropriate training for all their coaches, volunteers and club members. This will enable them to work together with parents/carers and other organisations to ensure that the needs and the welfare of young people remain paramount.

This is the RFU's own policy to do all it can to protect young children and to ensure that its coaches, trainers, and volunteers understand and carry out this policy. This means you. The RFU's policy recognises that you are at the sharp end and that protecting and looking after children in a positive and enjoyable way can only work if you play your part.

So what does my school or club have to do?

Schools will have their own measures for dealing with child protection, but there's no reason why teachers shouldn't check out the measures below and compare them with their own school's policy. If you are a coach and starting up a club, or even if you're an established club, you need to:

- read, understand and act upon what's in this chapter.

- if practical and possible, appoint a welfare officer who will act as the first point of contact for concerns about the welfare of young people (see Appendix 2 of the RFU's Guidelines for 'Terms of Reference').

- accept that all officers and committee members have a responsibility in this area and be prepared to respond to any indication of poor practice or abuse.

- put in place structures and systems to ensure that this is followed in practice.

- adopt and implement a 'best practice' policy for all adults working with young people (see the Fair Play Codes in the appendix).

- ensure that all relevant members who have regular supervisory contact with children or a management responsibility for those working with young people undertake a Disclosure and Barring Service check.

What to look out for?

EMOTIONAL ABUSE

In a rugby situation, emotional abuse may occur when coaches:

- provide repeated negative feedback: 'I see you played like a drain as usual, Johnny.' 'If you pass like that in our games, Donna, we'll lose all of them.'

- repeatedly ignore a young player's efforts to progress: 'She's not worth helping. She'll never get any better.'

- repeatedly demand performance levels above those of which the young player is capable: 'you'll stick at this until you get it right.'

- overemphasise the winning ethic: 'I don't want to see any losers in my teams. We're here to win.'

ABUSE BY NEGLECT

In a rugby situation, neglect may occur when:

- young players are left alone without proper supervision.

- a young player is exposed to unnecessary heat or cold without fluids or protection.

- a young player is exposed to an unacceptable risk of injury.

PHYSICAL ABUSE

In a rugby situation, physical abuse may occur when coaches, managers or helpers expose young players to:

- exercise or training that disregards the capacity of the player's immature and growing body.

- overplaying, overtraining or fatigue.

SEXUAL ABUSE

In a rugby situation, sexual abuse may occur when the close proximity of coaches and others to young people provides opportunities for potential abusers to exploit their position of trust to sexually abuse.

POOR PRACTICE

Poor practice includes behaviour that contravenes any of the following:

- Fair Play Codes (see the appendix at the back of this book).

- Good Practice in the Rugby Setting (contained in *Policy and Procedures for the Welfare of Young People in Rugby* to be found on the RFU website as a downloadable PDF document).

- Welfare and Procedures Policy for Young People (contained in *Policy and Procedures for the Welfare of Young People in Rugby* to be found on the RFU website as a downloadable PDF document).

BULLYING

It is of paramount importance that all rugby clubs have in place an anti-bullying policy to which all players, coaches and parents subscribe. Bullying is not always easy to define or identify and will not always be an adult abusing a young person; it is often the case that the bully is a young person. There are three main types of bullying.

Physical

For example, hitting, kicking or theft. Physical abuse among children can sometimes be hard to notice because it's often done slyly, when the coach or teacher isn't looking. Encourage victims or onlookers to let you know when it's happening. Do not allow a 'bystander' culture where children see bullying but do nothing about it. Remember that theft can also include extortion, such as 'Give us a pound (or drink, sweets and so on) and I'll leave you alone.'

Verbal

For example, racist or homophobic remarks such as 'stupid black kid', 'nutty Muslim' or 'you're gay'.

Emotional

For example, persistent negative feedback such as 'useless idiot', or 'you couldn't catch a ball properly if you had Velcro gloves on' or 'you lot were useless today, utter rubbish.'

All of these will include:

- deliberate hostility and aggression towards a victim or group.

- a victim who is weaker and less powerful than the bully or bullies.

- an outcome that is always painful and distressing for the individuals.

Bullying behaviour may also include:

- other forms of violence, such as intimidation, barging or tripping up. This may not necessarily occur on the field of play; very often it's in the changing rooms.

- sarcasm, spreading rumours and persistent teasing. Sarcasm and spreading rumours are never acceptable, but sometimes teasing forms part of a healthy friendship, such as light banter, a joke and a laugh between friends. However, when it becomes persistent, nasty and hurtful it must be stopped.

- tormenting, ridiculing or humiliation. There is no excuse for this behaviour by adults in charge of children, but among the children themselves this form of bullying often goes on in changing rooms or other areas where the children congregate without the adults being around. Be vigilant. Do spot checks and encourage players to come to you in confidence if this is occurring.

- graffiti or gestures. Graffiti of any kind, anywhere, is antisocial and vandalises property. It may include writing on another player's sports kit or bag. It's not cool and should not be tolerated. Gestures too can say as much as words and must be stopped if they are used to intimidate, criticise or humiliate anyone, whether child or adult.

- unwanted physical contact or abusive, offensive comments of a sexual nature. The competitive nature of rugby union makes it a potential environment for the bully. Snuff it out in your club or school.

WHAT TO LOOK FOR OUTSIDE YOUR CLUB OR SCHOOL

Be aware of potential abuse outside your tag rugby club or school, but note that such indicators as untreated injuries, seemingly overenthusiastic coaches, children who appear withdrawn, and so on, are not necessarily proof that a young person is being abused. Sometimes changes in behaviour can relate to other significant events in a young person's life, such as bereavement, internal family difficulties or bullying. Working in partnership with parents and carers and ensuring positive communication between everyone will help to ensure that reasons for changes in behaviour can be identified and action taken to support the young person.

WHAT TO DO IF YOU HAVE SUSPICIONS ABOUT ANY KIND OF ABUSE WITHIN THE CLUB OR SCHOOL

This includes anything listed above. If you have suspicions, follow the procedures as laid out in the RFU, RFUW and the NSPCC's *Policy and Procedures for the Welfare of Young People in Rugby Union*. It is *not* the responsibility of those working in rugby union to decide that abuse is occurring, but it *is* their responsibility to act on any concern. Non-action is not an option. The welfare of the young person or persons is paramount. Once the RFU Ethics and Equity Manager is informed, the RFU will take action and you can step back, having done your duty.

Health and safety

Remember to implement the following:

- **no contact**: ensure that the players understand the difference between the very physical nature of senior rugby and the non-contact element of tag rugby, and explain why.

- **safe environment**: ensure that players are safe from physical, emotional and sexual harm.

- **first aid**: having a basic knowledge of first aid will help to deal with the injury and assess whether it is minor or serious.

Also be aware of the following:

- **disability**: be aware of simple measures for coping with disabilities such as epilepsy or diabetes.

- **children in wheelchairs**: this has been dealt with in detail in Chapters 3–6.

- **children with learning difficulties**: be aware of the need for extra care for children who may have Down's syndrome and other such disabilities, but don't be fearful of these children playing tag rugby.

- **a real emergency**: serious injury in tag rugby is rare, but if it happens don't panic. Know what to do and when to summon an ambulance.

DBS

The DBS (Disclosure and Barring Service) has replaced the former CRB (Criminal Records Bureau). The DBS was formed by merging aspects of the Criminal Records Bureau and the Independent Safeguarding Authority (ISA) under the Protection of Freedoms Act 2012.

The new governing body provides wider access to criminal record information through its Disclosure Service for England and Wales. It also makes independent barring decisions on people in England, Wales and Northern Ireland who have previously harmed a child or vulnerable adult, or where there is a risk of harm from them to a child or vulnerable adult within the workplace or volunteer setting. Obviously, the volunteer setting is relevant to tag rugby as the overwhelming majority of coaches will be volunteers, and although sports teachers are paid for their work they too may involve themselves in volunteer work outside school hours.

Note that it is illegal for anyone barred by the DBS to work, or apply to work, with children or adults in the sector from which they are barred. It is also illegal for a rugby club to knowingly allow such a barred person to be involved in any capacity, coaching or other such activity, where young children are in their care.

By using the DBS service, organisations in the public, private, and voluntary sectors can make safer recruitment decisions by identifying candidates who may be unsuitable for certain work, especially work that involves children. This is particularly relevant to tag rugby for the Under 7s. The DBS also works to ensure unsuitable people do not work with vulnerable groups.

There is an online service which radically improves the ease and speed of making criminal record checks, and which will result in significant savings compared with the previous system. For £13 a year, applicants subscribing to this optional service can reuse their DBS Certificate when changing jobs or roles within the same sector. Where an individual has subscribed, an instant, online free check can be made to ensure that the existing certificate is up to date.

For all rugby clubs and schools this streamlined system should create real peace of mind regarding the safety of young children in their care, and the suitability of the individuals who coach or teach them.

Data Protection Act (DPA) 1998

This is very important legislation and clubs are required to adhere to the DPA. Data refers to any personal information kept by a club or school which must, among other requirements, be kept securely and fairly. Personal details will include name, address, date of birth, parents or carers and so on, and also refers to anything done with such data. For example, your club may want to organise and adapt it, store or delete it, or retrieve it. Protecting these details from misuse or carelessness should be given high priority especially when such personal details can be used illegally if they fall into the wrong hands. Remember too that anyone whose personal data you use has the right to see what you have processed about them.

BUT REMEMBER ...

Don't think that this all sounds too much like doom and gloom. The vast majority of children are well looked after by their parents or carers and you may never encounter any of the problems detailed above. Remember to be on your guard, know what to look for and how to act on it and then go and enjoy your rugby along with all the players.

10 FUNDING AND FESTIVALS

Starting a club is one thing; funding it and keeping it going is another. You will need basic equipment such as size 3 rugby balls, tag belts and markers, you may have to pay rent on a ground or clubhouse and you may also have other expenses such as electricity and heating. One of the most effective ways of funding is to have a subscription charge for all players, payable at the beginning of each season. Minis at Salisbury, for example, pay a sub which also covers insurance for the players. If you join in with an established club you will, of course, cut your costs by being able to share the expenses.

Alternatively, you could run your own fundraising events. There are many festivals and competitions already in place for tag rugby players, clubs and schools, but there's nothing to stop you from running one of your own. However, in order to do this it is essential that you prepare thoroughly before any other teams enter your grounds. There is also a wide variety of national and local funding agencies that can provide support for your school or club's project or needs (see pages 157–165).

Fundraising events

Festivals, competitions and fundraising events are fundamental to the lifeblood of a club or school. You could run your own tag rugby festival or cup competition, or have an event such as a barbecue, quiz night, bring-and-buy sale or Christmas party. Most important of all, events like this are great fun and bring people together for a common purpose. Social networks are established, friendships are made and clubs and school teams are strengthened.

HOW DO WE STAGE ONE?

The most efficient and successful way to run or take part in events is to set up an events committee. Schools can call on parents' associations as well as the school's own resources, and clubs will have social committees and members who are willing and able to help out. This leaves playing and training to the teachers and coaches, who have enough to do without operational aspects and fundraising.

SETTING UP A COMMITTEE

Any event, whether it's a barbecue or a local tag rugby festival, needs to be planned well in advance and will require lots of people with different talents and expertise. This means that the workload and responsibilities can be shared and will not depend on one driven person. Make sure that each member of the committee knows what his or her role is. This will maximise efficiency and ensure that the same task isn't duplicated by those who have no idea what other people are doing. Don't fall into the trap of having too many chiefs. Have one person in overall charge and make this clear to other members of the committee. Full cooperation is essential. The event director does not have to be the chair of the committee, nor does it have to be the same person each time. Choose the person who has the most experience and interest in that particular event. The events committee could also co-opt members of other committees in your club or school, such as the social committee, who can take care of catering, publicity and so on.

The following is a recommended committee structure, but is not written in stone.

You may want to adapt it to your particular circumstances.

- **Event director**: oversees the whole event.

- **Festival/competition manager**: organises all aspects of the structure of the event.

- **Promotions manager**: responsible for publicity and sponsorship.

- **Site manager**: responsible for all equipment and facilities needed on the day.

- **Volunteer manager**: recruits potential volunteers and coordinates their duties.

- **Treasurer**: someone trustworthy and knowledgeable about accounting.

The event director:

- oversees the whole event.

- is the person most qualified to run this particular event.

- determines how the event is to be run.

- makes the final decisions on event developments.

The festival/competition manager:

- sends out entry forms and covering letters to schools, clubs, companies and colleges.

- organises the structure of the event, who will play who, times, pitch and referee.

- organises referees, scorekeepers and other personnel needed for the day.

- gets the event covered by insurance.

- sends out event programmes and relevant information to participants.

The promotions manager:

- seeks sponsors, at sites such as www.uksponsorship.com/spt1.htm, and also look at awards for all funding (see end of this chapter for more information).

- produces the programme.

- informs the media.

- produces certificates.

- organises trophies and medals.

- designs a T-shirt for volunteers and referees, if funds allow.

The site manager:

- makes sure all equipment needed is provided, including size 3 rugby balls, tags and tag belts.

- ensures all facilities are in place.

- produces score desks.

- oversees marking of the pitches.

- organises a first-aid station and officer.

- organises refreshments.

- organises a public address system and/or two-way radios.

- is responsible for display boards.

- oversees entertainment.

The volunteer manager:

- provides a focal point for volunteers.

- attends events, festivals and socials to encourage and stimulate interest in new volunteers.

- recruits potential volunteers.

- welcomes new volunteers and keeps them informed of relevant information.

- coordinates the volunteer workforce throughout the event.

WHAT TYPE OF EVENT SHOULD WE HAVE?

You need to do the following:

- decide which type of event suits your club/school best, where it will take place and who will take part in it.

- decide what is to be achieved from the event.

- make sure you can fund it. Look at the suggestions for grants and awards on pages 163–164, which may cover some of your costs.

- choose a date and time that doesn't clash with something similar in your area.

- make sure that you have enough personnel/volunteers free to cover the entire event.

- involve parents/carers and other members of your school or club.

It is usual to award trophies or cups for events and tournaments so have a look at this website for more information:

www.trophies2u.co.uk

POINTS TO REMEMBER BEFORE YOU START

- **Treasurer**: you must set a budget and stick to it.

- **Promotions manager**: it's your job to generate as much publicity as possible so that you get the required number of players and people involved to make this a fantastic success.

- **Coordinators**: you must ensure that the venue is suitable and has disabled access.

Free stuff!

The promotions manager should try to get as much for free as he or she can by approaching potential sponsors for catering, prizes and publicity. What can you offer potential sponsors in return for their financial support or free goods? If you can offer something worthwhile, they will support the event. Examples of what you could offer include:

- advertising space at the club, particularly on match days.

- the chance to display merchandise: a car dealer could bring along one of the latest models to park and display at the club, which could lead to test drives or orders.

- publicity in the local newspaper, any relevant magazines and other similar publications.

- official acknowledgement as a supporter of the club.

- free or discount tickets for match events (especially at clubs like Harlequins).

- the chance for others to see you're a good citizen!

Funding

There is a wide variety of national and local funding agencies that can provide support for your club's project. In general, this funding support will either be in the form of revenue (people and projects) or capital (facilities and equipment).

HOW CAN I FIND FUNDING?

Contact your RFU Rugby Development Officer (RDO) for advice, and look at the information below on organisations that provide funding. You will also need to work out your 'three Os':

1. **Objective** – what do you aim to achieve?

2. **Output** – how will you deliver it?

3. **Outcome** – what difference will your project make?

Most importantly, do your homework! Thoroughly research the funding organisations and make sure the one you choose is the right one for your project. This is extremely important because you may have a very good case for a grant, but if you approach the wrong organisation it will not consider your application and it will all have been a hugely disappointing waste of time, skills and money. So, choose the funding organisation wisely, prepare your case really well and go for it!

How to get started

- Send out covering letters with details of the event and application forms to your target schools, clubs or organisations.

- Have a small flyer/poster to include with the covering letters, which will make the event very attractive to your targets.

- Decide on the fee level for entry into the competition or event.

- Book referees and organise scorekeepers and other personnel needed for the day.

- Make sure the event is covered by insurance.

- Have a great time!

ENGAGING A PROFESSIONAL FUNDRAISER

It's possible that your case will be better presented and have a greater chance of success if you use a professional fundraiser, but this will cost you so make sure that you have a good chance of being successful.

SOURCES OF FUNDING

Here are some sources of application for funding. It is not an exhaustive list and sometimes a particular source may cease to operate for one reason or another. **Note:** these websites and organisations change from time to time so they may not be in action when you read this book. You can always use a search engine to find them. Also look at what other clubs have achieved in the Community Rugby section on the RFU website, or use a search engine to find a club in your area.

The Rugby Football Foundation www.rfu.co.uk

The Rugby Football Foundation invests in community rugby facilities via the Community Rugby Capital Fund. The overall aim of the scheme is to finance capital projects to improve facilities and contribute to the recruitment and retention of community rugby players. All clubs at levels 5 and below in the English Clubs Rugby Union Championship (i.e. the leagues) are eligible to apply to the fund. For further information, visit www. rugbyfootballfoundation.org.

Awards for All

Awards for All is a Lottery grants scheme aimed at local communities. It awards grants to voluntary sports organisations such as rugby clubs, schools or colleges linking with local clubs, voluntary groups, disability groups, women's organisations, ethnic community groups and neighbourhood associations playing or planning to play sport. You can apply all year round and there are no deadlines. For more information visit www.awardsforall.org.uk.

The Big Lottery Fund

The Big Lottery Fund funds charities and the voluntary sector within sport. The fund focuses on smaller grants at local level and big capital projects, intended to regenerate and revitalise communities. For further information, visit www.biglotteryfund.org.uk.

The Coalfields Regeneration Trust

The Coalfields Regeneration Trust is an independent grant-making body registered with the Charity Commission and dedicated to the regeneration of the coalfield communities. For further information, visit www.coalfields-regen.org.uk.

Government grants

Voluntary and community organisations have access to £182 million of government funding. For further information, visit www.governmentfunding.org.uk.

Local authorities

The amount of funding available and the organisations that qualify will vary from one authority to another. Most have their own websites and phone numbers can be found in local directories.

National Association for Voluntary and Community Action

For further information, visit www.nacva.org.uk.

Sport England and UK Sport – Community Investment Fund

Rugby union is one of the most important sports to which Sport England and UK Sport will give priority for funding. Both these organisations are sponsored by the government. Decisions about Sport England funding and grants can be made locally by the nine regional sports boards. For further information, visit:

www.sportengland.org/funding or www.uksport.gov.uk.

FUNDRAISING SUPPORT

The following web-based agencies can provide software and support to your club, and can help locate suitable funding agencies in your local area:

- www.acf.org.uk – Association of Charitable Foundations.
- www.sportandrecreation.org.uk – Central Council for Physical Recreation.
- www.charitychoice.co.uk – an encyclopaedia of charities on the internet.
- www.fundinginformation.org – up-to-date information on funding sources.
- www.sportslink.info – online funding listings.

APPENDIX: THE RFU'S FAIR PLAY CODES

These codes are very helpful for the smooth running of a club or matches. There are codes for coaches, players, parents/carers, spectators and match officials. They can be photocopied and given out to the appropriate groups.

The good coach's code

In rugby union, coaches of young players should:

- Recognise the importance of fun and enjoyment.

- Realise that most learning is achieved through doing.

- Appreciate that the needs of the players come before the needs of the sport.

- Be a positive role model.

- Foster a good sports attitude and keep winning and losing in perspective.

- Respect all refereeing decisions and ensure that your players do the same.

- Discuss your team's performance with them in a positive way, which will encourage them; criticism will crush their spirit.

- Adjust coaching to the level of the young players' experience, physique, physical abilities and mental development.

- Ensure a safe environment, with adequate first aid.

- Use a squad system to avoid overuse of the best players and to ensure that all players get a chance to play.

- Never allow a player to train or play when injured.

- Ensure good supervision of young players, both on and off the field.

- Ensure that young players do not train or play in extremes of heat or cold, or where there is unacceptable risk of injury.

- Develop an awareness of nutrition and communicate this to young players as part of their lifestyle management.

- Ensure that their coaching keeps up to date with RFU codes and rules.

- Know and adhere to the policies and procedures outlined in the RFU Child Protection Guidance Booklet.

The good parent's and carer's code

Parents/carers are encouraged to:

- Be familiar with the coaching and training programme and keep it in the diary.

- Ensure your child is fully involved in the club or team.

- Let coaches know if your child can't get to a session.

- Become involved and offer assistance or expertise.

- Help coaches all you can with supervising the players.

- Offer transport to away games.

- Let the coaches know if you have any concerns.

- Support the good coach's code.

Parents/carers should also know that:

- Coaches should recognise the importance of fun and enjoyment for young players.

- Winning and losing is part of the game and players should be encouraged to accept both with dignity and praise for all players.

Parents/carers should:

- Show appreciation that all coaches, helpers, referees and other officials give up their precious free time for your child's enjoyment.

- Remember that rugby is primarily for the child's enjoyment, not just yours.

- Always encourage a child to play, but never force them.

- Focus on effort rather than winning or losing.

- Be aware of a child's capabilities and don't push them towards a level they won't be able to achieve.

- Provide positive comments in training and during the game.

- Be aware that negative comments undermine everyone's confidence and are unpleasant.

- Support the club or school in not tolerating loud or abusive behaviour from anyone, players or spectators.

- Respect decisions made by the match officials and encourage all children to do the same.

- Be a good role model.

The good player's code

Players are encouraged to:

- Appreciate the efforts made by coaches, assistants, match officials and administrators in providing the opportunity for you to play tag rugby.

- Have loyalty and commitment to the adults and your team-mates.

- Know that you have the right to be in a safe environment free from all types of abuse from adults and fellow team players.

- Know that you have the right to tell an adult, who belongs to the club or school or is outside of it, if you feel that you are not being treated properly by an adult or fellow team players.

Players should:

- Play because you want to, not because your coach or parents want you to.

- Realise that improving your skills and fun and enjoyment of the game are more important than winning or losing.

- Pay attention at training sessions.

- Work as hard for the team as you do for yourself.

- Be a good sport – win or lose.

- Play to the rules of tag rugby and accept, without any argument, all referees' decisions.

- Not allow your emotions to result in your physically or verbally abusing your team-mates, opponents or match officials.

- Treat everyone with respect in the way that you'd like to be treated yourself.

The good spectator's code

Spectators are encouraged to:

- Act as positive role models to all young players.

- Abide by the RFU Guidelines for Working with Children.

- Support the club or school in not tolerating loud or abusive behaviour from anyone, players or other spectators.

Spectators should:

- Remember that participation in sport is for the child's enjoyment.

- Accept that your enjoyment comes from theirs.

- Be sporting towards other teams.

- Respect match officials' decisions and remember that they are volunteers giving up their time so that the children can play tag rugby.

- Never verbally abuse anyone involved in the game as it undermines both officials and players and provides a negative role model for players to copy.

- Shout to encourage the players, not moan at them.

- Encourage all players regardless of their ability.

- Remember that ridicule is cruel and destructive.

The good match official's code

Match officials should:

- Recognise the importance of fun and enjoyment for young players.

- Comment in a constructive and encouraging way during games.

- Uphold the spirit of the game.

- Put the needs of young players before the needs of the sport.

- Understand the physical, social and emotional development of young children.

- Be a positive role model by setting a good example.

- Progress within the game by participating in courses such as Mini/Midi or National 15-a-side.

Match officials must:

- Recognise that the safety of young players is paramount.

- Explain decisions as all young players are continuing to learn.

- Always penalise foul play.

- Play advantage whenever possible in order to let the game flow.

- Show that you understand the age and ability of young players.

- Be consistent and objective.

- Ensure that verbal abuse from players, coaches or spectators is not tolerated and is dealt with by club officials immediately.

- Be aware of and abide by the RFU Child Protection Guide.

INDEX